Praise for The Truth About Identity Theft

"In an age when identity theft will affect everyone sooner or later, this book is simply a must-read. Jim Stickley teaches you to spot the danger signs and offers smart solutions for everything from banking security and online shopping scams to medical identity theft. Whether it's you, your parents', or your kids' identities, everyone has something to protect. This book tells you what you nee to k ow."

Producer, *The Today Show*

"Nowadays, identity theft is an   puts more than s finances in jeopardy. Fortunately, Jim Stickley's easy-to-understand advice can teach y how to spot and stay ahead of security threats. In short, this book is a must read."

Wes Millar, Senior Vice President of CUNA Strategic Services

"Jim Stickley shares his amazing experiences as a professional hacker in the most entertaining manner. He's a great storyteller and captures your attention with his experiences, which will make you want to upscale your efforts to protect your firm's data and your own ID. Jim's stories are fascinating. Most of us can't imagine how simple it is for him to succeed as a conman in situations we think are safe. The trade secrets of hackers he shares with us are mind boggling! You won't let your guard down after learning what Jim has actually done to get companies and individuals' private information. He's the updated version of 'To Catch a Thief'...but he's a good guy!"

Nancy E. Sheppard, President & CEO of Western Independent Bankers
(A Trade Association of 350 Banks)

"While Jim Stickley uses provocative means to garner his knowledge, much of his advice is indispensable. Anyone who has gone through the long, costly process of identity theft will tell you that taking some of these simple steps can help avoid a major headache down the road."

Lauren LaCapra, Personal-Finance Reporter, TheStreet.com

"As someone whose job involves stealing confidential information, Jim Stickley knows how easy it is for ID thieves to pilfer sensitive data. This must-read book offers insider tips for business owners and consumers seeking to protect themselves."

Leslie McFadden, reporter, Bankrate.com

"If you're not worried about identity theft, you should be...and Stickley tells you exactly why. His engaging writing style, coupled with real-life stories about identity theft and concrete actions to help you prevent identity theft, are exactly what's needed to make people take notice of this growing crime. I'll recommend this book again and again!"

Jerri L. Ledford, About.com Guide to Identity Theft

"*The Truth About Identity Theft* makes me want to take myself off the grid and live in a log cabin somewhere. Like most people, I thought I was fairly vigilant in protecting my identity, but I've learned a hundred new ways in which I am vulnerable to identity theft. While we have to live with it, Jim explains that we don't have to give in to it."

Peter Henning, Professor of Law, Wayne State University Law School

"What Jim Stickley knows about identity theft and how the bad guys can latch onto your digital information is essential. *The Truth About Identity Theft* is filled with an insider's mastery of this worsening problem. It provides a treasure chest of very useful information that will keep your identity out of harm's way. This book is absolutely required reading for anyone who has ever used a personal or public computer. What you don't know about identity theft can put you in the poorhouse."

Jack M. Germain, Technology Journalist for ECTNews Network and Linux.com

"Jim Stickley has years of experience probing the defenses of Fortune 500 companies. His expertise will help you create your own defenses against would-be identity thieves and scam artists."

Dave Nielsen, Founder of Fight Identity Theft.com

"Jim Stickley's book will not only surprise you in showing how simple it is for thieves to commit identity theft, but will also teach you to think about protecting yourself on a whole new level.

Are you afraid of identity theft yet? You should be. Jim Stickley shows you not only how easy it is to get your information, but how disastrous it is when that information gets used by thieves.

Identity theft is not something YOU have to worry about, right? WRONG. Jim Stickley shows you the sad truths about how easily your identity can be stolen, and his book gives you the mindset you will need in order to protect yourself.

Be glad Jim Stickley is a good guy and not an identity thief, because if he were, none of us would be safe. Unfortunately, there are many thieves just as smart as Jim. However, by reading his book, you can finally figure out how to protect yourself against this heinous crime."

Jonathan Kraft, Founder of www.IdentityTheftSecrets.com

THE TRUTH ABOUT
IDENTITY THEFT

Jim Stickley

Publisher
Paul Boger

Associate Publisher
Greg Wiegand

Acquisitions Editor
Rick Kughen

Development Editor
Rick Kughen

Technical Reviewer
"Wild Bill" Stanton

Marketing Coordinator
Judi Taylor

Cover and Interior Designs
Stuart Jackman,
Dorling Kindersley

Managing Editor
Kristy Hart

Senior Project Editor
Lori Lyons

Copy Editor
Karen A. Gill

Design Manager
Sandra Schroeder

Compositor
Gloria Schurick

Proofreader
San Dee Phillips

Manufacturing Buyer
Dan Uhrig

Library of Congress Cataloging-in-Publication Data on file.

Dedicated to the entire crew of TraceSecurity,
whose talents never cease to amaze me.

Introduction

I have stolen credit cards, hacked social security numbers, robbed banks, and created fake ATMs. I have broken into armed government facilities and have stolen from teenagers. I am an identity thief, but I am no criminal.

In the end, I have found there is little separation between attacking a corporation in New York City and targeting a housewife in Dover, Ohio.

> I am an identity thief, but I am no criminal.

Fortunately for all victims involved, I was hired to perform these attacks by corporations testing their security, news agencies investigating security concerns, and other media outlets interested in knowing just how easy it is to commit identity theft. My job is to find security flaws before the real criminals find them.

> My job is to find security flaws before the real criminals find them.

This book has been designed to give you the insight that most people experience only after becoming victims of identity theft. Each Truth walks you through a different type of attack, explaining the complete process in a simple and straightforward way.

Like a magician actually revealing what happens behind the curtain, I take you through the attacks to reveal how people at home, work, and on the road become victims. I identify tips on how to protect yourself, your office, and your children from becoming the next identity theft statistics.

Identity thieves can, and often do, use all the attacks against any type of target, regardless of whether they are after you in your home in the Midwest or if they are targeting you in your New York City office. While learning to think like an identity thief, you will begin to look at situations in an entirely new way. You might think twice about that preapproved credit card application that arrived in the mail, and you might keep a closer eye on that pest inspector who has spent just a little too much time walking around your office. Ultimately, this book opens your eyes to a world most people never knew existed.

There is no doubt that I have had to walk a fine line when performing the attacks that I outline in this book. On one hand, I am hired by organizations to conduct these tests; on the other hand, I am stealing the confidential information of millions of unsuspecting individuals. In the end, the information I steal ends up being far more secure than before I touched it, and the lessons learned have benefited hundreds of thousands of others in their efforts to avoid being the next identity theft victims. Of course, there have been engagements that were flat-out illegal. In those cases, the proper authorities were notified ahead of time, and although the attacks were real and unrehearsed, I had my "get out of jail free" paperwork.

> In this day and age, what you don't know is exactly what can hurt you.

In this day and age, what you don't know is exactly what can hurt you. Identity thieves are out there, and their success often comes from innocent mistakes made by others.

TRUTH

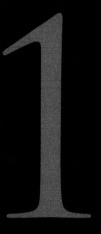

Phishing scams

Identity thieves have been attacking unsuspecting computer users since the late 1990s. Often, these attacks come through bogus emails that appear to have been sent by local banks, credit unions, online auction services, credit card companies, and just about every other online service. The ultimate goal of these attacks is to gain access to your confidential information. The attacks are known as *phishing*, and identity thieves have become slick with them. Identity thieves continue to thwart the efforts of security companies that attempt to detect and prevent consumers from falling victim to phishing attacks.

The main issue with trying to prevent these types of attacks is that it is difficult to prove where an email originated. Anyone can send an email and use a fake email return address (called *spoofing*). This is no different from your writing a letter, signing it Bob Hope, and mailing it to a friend. The recipient has no way of knowing who really sent it. The same thing is true with email.

In addition to spoofing email, identify thieves can include a URL in the email that directs you to click the link to validate your account. Of course, this link goes to a phishing Web site that resides on one of the thousands of free Web hosting sites on the Internet. These sites are located all around the world and do not track information about who set up the Web pages or how to track them down. Anyone can make a Web site and, more importantly, anyone can mimic a real site. This is where many people get sucked in. You see the PayPal logo and automatically think you have arrived at the PayPal site. Instead, you've just been lured to a fake site, and if you enter any of your personal information, you can expect it to be a costly error.

> You have to use a certain amount of common sense and a large amount of paranoia.

Now, obviously if you don't have a PayPal account, a fake email from PayPal is going to be quite obvious. But what happens when the bogus email appears to have come from your financial institution? Do you click on the link embedded in the email and provide your confidential information?

Unfortunately, emails asking you to click a link in an email and enter confidential information aren't always phishing schemes. In fact, sometimes they are perfectly legitimate. In the past few years, I have seen many organizations send emails that are similar to emails sent by identity thieves. Some credit card companies send legitimate email offers that require you to follow a link to a Web site

It's no wonder identity thieves are having such success when legitimate organizations are perpetuating a flawed system.

and enter confidential information. It's no wonder identity thieves are having such success when legitimate organizations are perpetuating a flawed system.

So how do you avoid becoming another phishing victim statistic? In the end, you have to use a certain amount of common sense and a large amount of paranoia.

- Pay attention to the email addressee. If it does not include your complete name, you cannot trust the content of the email. Be aware, however, that emails containing your complete name can be fake, too. If there is any doubt, do not provide any information online. Call the institution and ask to speak to a customer service representative to determine if the email is legitimate.

- Pay attention to the Web address included in the email. After you click on the link, pay attention to the site that appears. Often, the URL will look correct in the email, but when your browser opens the Web page, it will be at a different address. Often it will end up at an IP address such as 10.0.0.1 instead of a typical Web address, such as www.paypal.com. If your browser ends up at either an IP address or at an address that just doesn't make sense, you should not trust the site.

- Never open an attachment in an email regardless of who sent it unless you were specifically expecting it and know what it is. I have broken into more computers through the use of attachments than any other means. Just opening the attachment is enough to compromise your entire computer.

3

Knowing how to protect yourself is important, but businesses also need to be doing their part to bring phishing to an end. Here are a few simple steps that every business should be following.

- Stop sending URLs in emails to your customers. This seems so logical, yet I continue to see marketing campaigns that include these links. Instead, simply suggest in the email that users visit your Web site and instruct them on a specific menu option they should select. This allows customers to take advantage of the offer included in the email, but it also trains them not to click links in emails.

- Get the word out. Warn your customers often about the risks of phishing attacks, and let them know you will never send links in your emails. People need to know what to expect, so they can recognize when something is suspicious.

- Just because your company has not been targeted by identity thieves for a phishing attack doesn't mean it won't be. Much like a disaster recovery plan, handling a phishing attack requires preparation. Here are some questions you need to be considering.

  - How will you get the phishing site taken down? A number of companies offer services to help take down phishing sites. Work out the cost ahead of time; you'll get a far better deal if you're not in a rush because you're currently under attack.

  - How will you notify your customers? Obviously, you want to warn people as soon as possible so that you reduce the number of victims. Will you do this through phone calls, emails, or notices on your own Web site?

  - What do you do about customers who have been compromised? Cancel their accounts? Freeze them? Are there ways to look for suspicious activity?

- Use personal identifiers. Some companies *must* send emails that contain URLs that users need to click. In these cases, allow users to set up a personal identifier word or phrase that you can include with your email to them. This allows users to recognize the word or phrase. If the personal identifier is not contained in the email, they know the email is fake.

TRUTH

2

Vishing attacks

Unlike phishing scams, which typically use phony Web sites to harvest your personal information for the purpose of identity theft, vishing is the practice of using analog phones or voice over IP (VoIP), along with some slick social engineering tactics, to steal identities. By combining the terms voice and phishing, you get vishing, the latest in a long line of ways enterprising thieves have devised to separate you from your hard-earned cash.

Because telephone calls conducted over the Internet allow for easy caller ID spoofing (read: an identity thief can pose as your banking institution and even appear to be calling from your bank), vishing is a particularly nasty approach to the growing identity theft problem.

In a typical vishing attack, the identity thief will call, posing as a representative from your bank, credit union, stock broker, or other financial institution. The typical scam involves the thief first leaving the victim an urgent voice message to call him back. When the victim returns the call, the thief employs an elaborate con in which the victim might be transferred to multiple "departments." Ultimately, the victim will be asked to give his name, primary account number, and, for security purposes, his social security number. One con is for the thief to tell the victim that a substantial charge has been made to his card (or something similar) and that the purpose of the call is to verify the charge. When the victim tells the thief that he didn't make the charge, the thief offers to remove it. Thus, the victim thinks he is averting an identity theft when, in actuality, the theft is occurring right over the phone.

> The victim thinks he is averting an identity theft when, in actuality, the theft is occurring right over the phone.

While this scenario takes time and requires the thief to be available to answer the call, this type of attack can be much less sophisticated and yet every bit as successful. Documented cases have shown up throughout the United States where people receive voice messages and emails asking them to call an 800 number to resolve some issue. The phone number left for the user to call is tied back to an automated attendant that allows the caller to enter information via touch tone. This information is gathered electronically via a computer, which can automatically be forwarded anywhere in the world, allowing the thief to remain anonymous.

I have performed this type of attack for financial institutions, health care facilities, and various other businesses. Their goal in trying these attacks is to train employees and customers on the risks of vishing. Of the hundreds of people tested, over 50% have given me at least their name and social security number, which is all that is needed to commit identity theft. In most cases, I was able to gain additional information, including account numbers, driver's license numbers, home addresses, and sometimes even a mother's maiden name.

People often ask how thieves obtained their phone numbers or email addresses. Because these types of attacks don't need to be specific to any one person, in most cases the numbers are dialed randomly. Automated software packages called *war dialers* simply dial one randomly generated phone number after another. With email, identity thieves have access to those same mailing lists that people use to send spam.

So how do you protect yourself from falling victim to this type of identity theft scam?

- Never give out confidential information over the phone when someone calls you. Unless you know the person or were expecting the call, there is no way for you to know who you are really speaking with.

- If you receive a message requiring you to return a call, don't use the number that's recorded on the voice mail. Even a toll-free number doesn't guarantee legitimacy. Instead, if the voice mail is purportedly from your financial institution, you should use the number listed on the back of your ATM, debit, or credit card. Otherwise, look up the number

Asking for your complete social security number is unacceptable and should be a red flag that you may be dealing with an identity thief.

7

in the phone book, or use directory assistance. This is a better guarantee that you are calling a legitimate company.

■ When you call an organization that requires you to validate who you are, the most the person on the other end should ever ask for is the last four digits of your social security number. Asking for your complete social security number is unacceptable and should be a red flag that you may be dealing with an identity thief.

Of course, organizations can also do their part to help reduce the number of successful attacks.

■ As with most identity theft issues, getting the word out is the most effective way of helping your customers. Most people have never heard of vishing attacks. A simple warning on your Web site or included with a monthly billing statement lets people know what it is and what to watch for.

■ When you are required to reach customers by phone, don't just stop at verifying that they are your customers. Make sure you verify who *you* are as well. Giving information, like part of the customers' account number, when their last bill was received, and the total of their last bill can help put a customer's mind at ease.

■ Create a unique identifier for each customer. You can then use this identifier when you contact that customer. Train your customers to expect that identifier to be used when anyone from your institution calls them and asks for information.

■ One of the best solutions is to stop using a social security number or even a part of a social security number as a means for user verification. Social security numbers were never meant to be your identity, yet that is what they have become. Allow your customers to choose their own security passwords and use them to verify who they are.

TRUTH

3

Phishing via snail mail

When you think of phishing, you probably think of the annoying emails you receive that request you to change your password on your PayPal account. They're annoying, and fortunately, they're starting to get easier to detect. However, what happens when the same tactics are used via the U.S. Mail? What if you received a letter from your bank that required you to fill out a form to validate your information and mail it back? It's easy to believe that you would be suspicious, but when I started actually testing people, I was surprised to see just how quick people were to give their confidential information.

You open your mailbox, and there's an envelope from your bank. Inside is a letter along with a separate questionnaire and a return envelope. The letter reads something to the effect of this.

Dear Jim,

Recently, several new federal regulations were released that require us to research and validate all customer account information. This effort is driven by the need for tighter security in the financial sector. Often times, errors caused by typos and other computer-related inconsistencies can cause accounts to contain inaccurate information. When left unchecked, numerous issues can arise, including the inadvertent bypass of certain state and federal taxes.

At ACME Bank, it is important to us that all our customers' data is 100% accurate, and to help ensure that we maintain this level, we are requiring all customers to take a moment to complete and return the included informational form.

This form will be used by ACME Bank service representatives to cross-reference against your existing account. If any discrepancies are discovered, you will be contacted, and changes will be made if necessary.

For your convenience, a special Web site has been set up to also allow for online filing. Simply visit http://www.acmebankupdates.com and select the option Account Verification located on the right side of the Web page.

After reading the letter, you look at the form that has been included. It has a place for you to fill in all the information required by the financial institution. This includes your name, address, phone number, social security number, driver's license number, and mother's maiden name. You take a few moments to complete the form and stick it in the return envelope. You drop it with your outgoing mail, and you don't give it another thought.

You might also be more technical, so instead of using the included form, you go to the Web site mentioned in the letter. The same information is required, so you complete it and submit the form.

During the past two years, I have run this attack numerous times and have always had success. From financial institutions to health care organizations, it is always the same. People fill out the information and send it back. There are cases where I get back only 10% of the forms sent out, but even more often I get back every single one. When I talk to the victims about it afterward, they generally come to the same conclusion. They get mail from that particular organization all the time, so this piece didn't seem like anything out of the ordinary. That's what makes being an identity thief so easy. People never know they are under attack because the attack blends in with day-to-day life.

> That's what makes being an identity thief so easy. People never know they are under attack because the attack blends in with day-to-day life.

Credit card applications by mail

Okay, you get it now. If a letter comes in the mail from your bank and it's asking for confidential information, you should probably ignore it. But what about that preapproved credit card application you received last week? Sorry, but I have had just as much success attacking unsuspecting individuals using credit card offers as I have with letters from the bank. It's actually pretty simple. There is not a week that goes by where I don't receive at least one preapproved credit card application in the mail. Some of them offer to give me free luggage if I sign up; others offer a great interest rate for the first 90 days. The one thing that every application seems to have in common is that I have never heard of the company that is offering them. Sure, it's a Visa or MasterCard, but what organization is actually sending out the card? The truth is, most people never pay attention.

I have sent out hundreds of these fake preapproved applications. I generally choose fake names for my credit card companies that sound similar to something people may have already heard of. In reality, I could just as easily use real company names, as no one would ever know the difference. Of course, I always offer low interest rates and, more importantly, a gift for signing up. On one of my attacks, I offered the Nintendo Wii, and over 50% of the recipients signed up. Of course, to sign up, the victims were required to submit their name, address, social security number, driver's license number, mother's maiden name, and email address. That is everything an identity thief would need to start a new life.

...name, address, social security number, driver's license number, mother's maiden name, and email address. That is everything an identity thief would need to start a new life.

It is difficult to tell a real credit card application from a fake. Therefore, I suggest you always err on the side of caution and never fill one out no matter how good the offer and how great the free gift. If you are looking for a credit card, talk to your friends and family members. Find out what cards they use and which cards have the best interest rates, and then call the 800 number located on the back of their credit cards. This will guarantee that you are truly getting involved with a real organization and not some guy sitting in his basement printing up credit card applications for kicks.

TRUTH

4

Spear phishing

By now, you know the basics of phishing. What you don't know, I'm betting, is that identity thieves routinely target employees of organizations that offer online services such as Web mail, virtual private networks (VPNs), or online banking. Since employees often carry the keys to the kingdom, identity thieves often attempt to go right to the source. The premise is still the same; send an email to an individual, and get that person to follow a link where he will submit confidential information into an online application. The difference is that when I go after the employees, I am using what some refer to as spear phishing.

Spear phishing is when you target a specific victim instead of setting an all-purpose trap for any victims who happen by. When spear fishing, the thief often poses as someone the victim trusts. For example, if an identity thief knows that an employee does her personal banking with a specific institution, the thief will send an email to her, addressing her by name on behalf of her bank. Or the identity thief can pose as someone that the victim knows and trusts, perhaps as a member of the corporate tech support group.

When I attack an employee at the office, the first thing I need is his email address. Most organizations do not make their employees' email addresses public, which means that I have to find them on my own. To start, I gather a list of all the employee names I can track down. To do that, I simply call the organization late at night, and when the voice mail system comes on, I select the option to give me the directory service. When the auto attendant prompts me to enter the first three characters of the employee's last name, I simply press the number 2, which is the a, b, and c key. After a few seconds, the system times out and starts listing all the names of every employee whose last name starts with the letter a, b, or c. I write down every name and then move on to the number 3 key to get d, e, and f.

I continue this tedious process until I have the name of every employee in that system. Of course, just having a name doesn't mean I have an email address...or does it? If you work at a company that is similar to just about every other company on the planet, I bet your email address has the same layout as everyone else you work with. For example, if your email is jane.doe@yourcompanyhere.com,

I would bet that your coworker has an email that is bill.smith@ yourcompanyhere.com. That's because most mail server software lets you assign what kind of algorithm you want to use for your company, and every new user receives an email address that matches that algorithm.

So to track down the email address, I simply attempt to send an email to every email version I can possibly think of. For example, if the user's name is Jane Doe, I would send an email to jane.doe@..., janedoe@..., jdoe@..., janed@..., and so on.

If you've ever mistyped an email address, you've noticed that within a minute of sending the letter, you receive an email back saying the user did not exist. This lets you know you made a mistake, and you can try again. Well, the same thing happens with the emails that I send. Within a minute or two, all the emails start bouncing back to me. That is, they all start bouncing back with the exception of one. Almost every time I try this, there will be one variation of the email address that doesn't bounce back. Why? Because that address turned out to be the user's real email address. So if jane.doe@ yourcompanyhere.com doesn't bounce back, then bill.smith, and every other first.last name will probably work as well. This means I now have a list of every user's email address at that company.

For this example, let's assume that I want to start finding out employees' user names and passwords for their online Web mail service. I would next call the main office and ask to speak to the IT network manager. When I reach that person, I would simply ask who I was speaking with and then tell the manager I am a vendor selling a product or service. Of course, the IT manager is likely to hang up on me, but I have the information I came for: the IT manager's name. And I already have his email address.

Before I send my phishing email, I create a simple Web site that looks similar to an online Web mail Web site.

Now for the fun part. Assuming that the IT network manager's name is Bill Smith, I spoof an email that will come from what looks like Bill Smith, and I will send it to as many employees as I feel like.

Hey <NAME HERE>,

I wanted to let you know we are putting up a new version of the Web mail. This new version should be faster, allow for better search capacities, and ultimately will tie in with everyone's cell phones.

When you have a second, can you try it out and let me know if you were able to get your email?

The link is http://192.168.1.1/webmail.

Thanks!

Bill Smith

I have done this spear fishing test with hundreds of employees throughout the United States and have over a 98% success rate. The employees receive the email, trust that it really was sent from Bill, and immediately follow the link with no questions asked. Of course, the users are prompted to enter their username and password, which I collect for use later. Often, I modify the return address so it is just a little different from Bill's real address, so if users reply, those replies will come to me instead of the real Bill Smith.

When I have a username and password, I can become any employee I want to be. I can read employees' email, send email on their behalf and, even more importantly, learn what systems they can access. I can then request password resets for those systems and have new passwords sent right to the users' email accounts, which, remember, I have hijacked.

For as complicated as this type of phishing attack actually is, the solution is the exact opposite. It is as easy as picking up the telephone. Email should not be used for everything. If you receive an email that requires you to submit any confidential information or allow potential access to confidential areas, simply pick up the phone, dial the extension of the person who sent the email, and say, "Hi. Did you just send me this email?" It truly is that simple. If the person denies sending the email, you or your IT department should sound the alarm.

TRUTH

One man's trash is another man's identity

Through the years, I have broken into numerous banks through hundreds of different attacks. Though each was different, the main objective was often the same: to gain access to the cash or confidential information. I was once approached by a large financial institution that was not only concerned about the security of its physical locations and its network, but also had concerns about the risks associated with upper management. This institution asked that I also investigate whether its management team could be attacked in a way that might allow an identity thief greater access to its organization.

So each afternoon I waited in the parking lot and watched members of the management team get into their vehicle. Then I followed them home. Within a couple of weeks, I had each of their home addresses. Since I had no permission to break into their homes and poke through their personal belongings, I opted for the next best thing: their garbage.

Through the years, I have been amazed at the things you can find in the trash. There is big business for identity thieves in personal garbage. More importantly, when you put your garbage out on the street for trash pickup, it usually becomes open to the public. This means that if I am so inclined, I can take that garbage and bring it home, which is exactly what I did. Each week I would snap on my rubber gloves and go through every item of trash: grocery store shopping lists, sticky notes with phone numbers, a private invitation for a little girl to a friend's birthday party, and much more. As I continued to go through the managers' trash, I was able to compile a list of their service providers: water bill, phone bill, gas and electric, cable, and so on. I could use this information not only to gain access into their lives but, if I wanted, to take over their lives.

I could use this information not only to gain access into their lives but, if I wanted, to take over their lives.

Ultimately, I decided to use the billing information for the bank managers' Internet service providers as an access point for my attack. Using the information I gained from the bills, I contacted the managers and explained that I was from that company. I told them that we were updating our services and that, for them to continue to have Internet service, they would be required to install updated software. I explained that the software would be arriving within the next week.

Because I was also able to reference their past billing information during the call, the victims never suspected a thing. Within a week, they each received a package in the mail that contained "upgrade software" and instructions. One by one, the managers installed the software.

Of course, the software they had just installed was actually malicious and designed specifically to allow me to access their computer via the Internet from anywhere in the world. Shortly after they installed the software, I was on their computers going through all their files. Within a few short days, I had usernames and passwords to corporate systems and even VPN access, which allowed me to connect directly to the financial institution's internal network.

When I submitted my report to the executives at the organization, they were obviously floored. None of them had ever suspected that I had targeted them at home, even though they had all signed waivers allowing me to do so. They said they were being cautious about emails that were being sent to them, as they were convinced that was how I was going to try to get in; but the idea that I would go through their trash and use that against them had never crossed their minds.

Now, you might be asking yourself what that story has to do with identity theft. Sure, I was able to gain access to that financial institution by attacking its employees at home, but technically the employee was never placed directly at risk, just the employer. In reality, those employees turned out to be far more vulnerable than I would have imagined. However, since I was not hired to test them personally, I just bypassed those opportunities and stayed focused on my primary target: the bank.

If you own a credit card, you are probably used to the clutter of junk mail that comes on behalf of the credit card company. While most of the junk included with your bill is harmless, the issue occurs when the credit card company decides to make it easier for you to spend money. Credit card checks have become a lucrative business for credit card companies. These checks can be used just like regular checks to pay anything from other credit card bills to buying food at the grocery store. Because you can use these checks in situations where credit cards would not have been accepted, they allow you a new freedom to continue to rack up credit card debt. These checks are often included with numerous other documents that are all stuffed into your monthly credit card statement.

While attacking the bank's management team, I found many of these checks still inside the opened statement envelope, which had been dropped in the trash. All I had to do was take these checks and go on a shopping spree.

There were other identity theft attack opportunities made available to me during these tests. Each bill that I found contained great information. For example, on the cable bill, the victim's name, address, and account number were available. In addition, I could see the total of the current bill, the amount of the previous bill, and if they paid it. Using just this information, I could call the victim, explain that I was from the cable company, and say that we had not received a payment for this month's bill. The victim, of course, would say he had paid it, and I would argue that he may have sent a check, but we had not received it, so it may be lost in the mail. I would explain that, though unfortunate, his service was being turned off and he would have to incur a fee to have it reenabled.

I would then offer the victim the ability to pay the bill via a credit card or check over the phone. I would explain that if his other payment did finally show up, it would be destroyed. Again, it is important to note that mentioning the victim's previous payment amount and when it was received helped lend me credibility. The victim would relent and give his credit card number or checking account number and bank routing number. Once complete, I could've simply taken that information and gone on a buying spree.

There is a simple solution to avoiding this kind of attack: Shred everything. I mean it. Everything! If you are throwing away any paper that contains personal information, shred it first. Shredders come in a few different types, but I highly recommend that you spend a little extra to make sure that it does cross-cut shredding and can shred CDs and credit cards. This type of shredder runs faster and shreds more items at a time, allowing you to spend less time standing in front of it.

Remember: One man's trash truly can be another man's treasure. Unfortunately, one man's treasure might actually be stolen from another man's identity. So start shredding.

TRUTH

6

Dumpster diving for profit

In the previous Truth, I spoke about what people throw away when they are at home and the risks that come with it. However, those risks are nothing compared to what my coworkers and I have discovered while dumpster-diving throughout the years. While many states have started prosecuting companies for discarding consumers' confidential information insecurely, it seems the majority of the world has simply not paid attention.

In early 2007, Radio Shack allegedly dumped more than 20 boxes containing private information for thousands of customers. A man rummaging through the dumpster found the boxes and reported it. In April, the State of Texas filed a civil law suit against Radio Shack for allegedly exposing its customers to identity theft. The suit claimed that the company "failed to safeguard the information by shredding, erasing, or other means, to make it unreadable or undecipherable before disposing of its business records."

The fact that the data was discovered comes as no surprise. The simple fact is that throughout the hundreds of dumpsters that I have had the pleasure of "visiting," it has been a rare day that I come away empty-handed. Most often I leave with enough confidential information to keep the average identity thief in business for months, or even years. I have found social security numbers, copies of drivers' licenses, credit applications, credit card numbers, complete names and addresses, and phone numbers—all in the trash. And those are just the obvious things.

A company we recently tested was actually throwing away the drug test documentation on all of its potential new hires. Each document included the name, address, social security number, and the results of the test. Not only was the company putting that person at risk of identity theft, but it was also a walking time bomb for a lawsuit. Imagine if one of those potential employees had failed that test and the information was made public? The fallout could have been devastating on all sides.

At another location, a financial institution was discarding confidential information, including copies of loan applications, social security numbers, banking account numbers, and more. But in this case, instead of placing the items in the trash dumpster, the institution was placing the information in bins located outside the facility designated for recycling. I have noticed that this seems to be part of a growing trend in confidential information leaks. In general, people are interested in the green movement, and instead of throwing items that need to be shredded into the appropriate designated shred areas, they are placing the documents into the recycle bin.

Recycling versus shredding

When I have spoken with employees who have been caught placing sensitive documents into recycling bins, their explanation has been that they thought recycling was different from trash and, therefore, somehow safe. When asked to explain further, employees generally tell me that, while trash ends up at the landfills where anyone could get his hands on it, recycling is taken to a place where it will be reused. They often tell me they feel that it's safe to place confidential documents into a recycling bin since the document will be destroyed instead of being shipped to a landfill. Let me be perfectly clear: Recycling is no more secure than throwing the items into the trash. For those out there who are worried about being green, most major shredding companies do recycle once they have shredded the documents.

> Recycling is no more secure than throwing the items into the trash.

What's your company line?

I have found that the amount of confidential information I discover in the garbage is directly related to how much the organization preaches the virtues of shredding to its employees.

My personal theory is this: Walk up to an employee's desk and stick your arm straight out like wings on an airplane. Now spin in a circle. Is there a place for the employee to place confidential documents that require shredding within your arm span? If not, I can promise you that the employees are probably not shredding everything they need to.

The problem is this: Often times an organization places a shred barrel on each floor of its facility. The employees are then expected to get up throughout the day and place any papers they have with confidential information on them into those bins. Of course, what ends up happening is that the employees begin to build a pile on their desks of questionable items. As the day goes on, the papers start to get in the way. Since the employees are busy and not willing to take the stack to the shred barrel, they often just put them in the trash or do what I refer to as the "poor man shred." That is, they physically tear up the paper themselves. When I find documents that have been torn by hand, I take them home and give them to my 7-year-old son and tell him it's a puzzle. He always puts them back together.

In other cases, if employees end up with only one document that needs shredded, they may not want to waste the trip to the shred barrel, so again, the document ends up in the trash.

Shredders for all

The best possible solution is to have a small shredder at each desk. This makes it easy for employees to shred every work paper, eliminating any confusion of what is and is not considered confidential. If that is not a feasible option, add a second trash can at each desk designated for shredding. If you choose this second option, be aware that it does come with additional risks. You must make certain that the recycling at each employee's desk is removed at the end of each day. You do not want to be leaving an open box of confidential documents at each desk where the cleaning crew or other visitors may have access.

My last suggestion is the most important. I highly recommend that you get yourself some rubber gloves and a couple of empty trash bags and head out to your own dumpster. Find out for yourself what is ending up in your trash. You will probably be amazed and possibly even a little concerned about what you find.

TRUTH

7

Your used computer is worth its weight in gold

Several years ago, I was working for a company that had sales reps located throughout the U. S. One day I received a call from a coworker who was extremely upset about a telephone call he had just received. A man in Las Vegas had called to inform him that he was looking at the files for a number of our corporate clients. In addition, he had access to several months' worth of corporate email and numerous other memos and proprietary information. While it sounded as if this man was trying to threaten our company, it turned out that he was just irritated at such a ridiculous breach in security and felt obligated to call and tell someone.

Several months earlier, another sales rep who had lived in Las Vegas purchased a personal laptop. While he actually owned the laptop, he used it to telecommute from home to the corporate office. Being a sales rep, he had access to numerous corporate files, email, customer accounts, and so on. After a couple of months, he decided that the laptop was no longer adequate. So he went back to the store where he purchased it and demanded a refund. Unbelievably, he got the refund and returned the computer to the store with all the confidential files still on it. All usernames and passwords saved on the system were left behind—emails, memos, files, documents, everything.

Each day, thousands of computers containing sensitive data end up being thrown in the trash or donated to individuals and organizations.

Now, one might think that this laptop would have been reformatted and returned to factory specs before being resold. It was clear that it had been used for several months. Unfortunately, however, the laptop was sold to another customer, still containing all the sales rep's confidential files.

I can only imagine the second owner's shock when he opened Outlook and it automatically logged into the corporate network and started downloading the sales rep's latest emails. Fortunately, the second buyer turned out to be honest, and the data on the system was ultimately destroyed. However, not everyone is so lucky and, more importantly, not every situation is quite so obvious.

Each day, thousands of computers containing sensitive data end up being thrown in the trash or donated to individuals and organizations. The problem is that often the computers are simply turned off and boxed up without any thought for the existing data still on the hard drives. These computers often don't end up in landfills. Instead, they get bundled together with other computers, placed on a pallet, and then sold in bulk at auctions for pennies on the dollar.

Identity thieves have been well aware of these practices for years and seek out auctions where these pallets of computers are being offered. They then take the computers home and, one by one, go through all the data located on the hard drives. Some people do realize the risks related to their hard drives and delete any confidential files before they turn them in. Unfortunately, thieves expect this, so in addition to just looking at the existing data, they run undelete software that goes through the hard drive and finds files that had previously been deleted.

Although the thieves are not guaranteed to gain confidential information in this manner, the risk-to-reward payoff is definitely in their favor. Even if just one computer contains just one person's confidential information, the identity thief will make far more than the small investment he paid for that pallet of computers.

Of course, it's not just computers that you give away. In other cases, thieves purchase old laptops and computers via sites such as eBay. These computers are often offered by both home users and large corporations. Again, the goal of the thief is to undelete any files on the computer when it arrives with the hopes of gaining information he can use to commit identity theft.

While identity theft is of major concern, there are also the legal issues that can come from data being left on the computer. For example, a lawyer leaving confidential case information on the hard drive could be worth its weight in gold to an identity thief. Again, just deleting the information doesn't mean that it's gone. If it were to end up in the wrong hands, the costs could be millions or even billions to the affected corporation.

Destroy your data before retiring a computer

While my suggestion is to simply destroy the hard drive (opening the drive and taking a hammer to the drive platters will do the trick) before disposing of a computer, you won't necessarily have this option if you are selling the computer. If you are selling a computer with the hard drive(s) still installed, the next best option is to reformat the hard drive using software designed to securely delete the data.

When you delete a file from a computer's hard drive, the file technically does not go away. Instead, the pointer record that shows where the file is located is removed, but the file itself remains. Over time, some or all of the files will be overwritten as newer programs are saved in its place. With small drives, this can happen quickly, but with large drives, this may take a much longer period of time. Numerous software applications have been designed to locate and undelete your deleted files. These programs are extremely easy to use and take just a few minutes to track down hundreds of previously deleted files.

There is software, however, that has been designed to securely wipe the selected files from the hard drive. In most cases, the software flags where the file was on the hard drive and then writes new data to that location multiple times. The more times it writes data to the previous file's location, the less likely someone can undelete the original file. Both free and corporate versions of these programs are available to permanently erase your data and software applications. Whereas the free versions may not be quite as user-friendly, they are generally just as secure.

It is easy for me to say that you should erase anything that is confidential; ultimately, that may prove harder than you think. Often, operating systems save data, including backups of what you are typing, while you are working on them. Even if you delete the primary file, the backup may still exist hidden away on your drive but easily found by the "undelete" software. For that reason, when possible, I suggest never giving your old computer with the hard drives still installed and intact to anyone who you cannot completely trust. And be sure you destroy your drives before tossing them into the trash.

TRUTH

8

Pickpockets and purse snatchers still exist

When you think of pickpockets, you might think of the artful dodger in *Oliver Twist*. But what you probably don't realize is that pickpockets still roam the streets today searching for unsuspecting men and women who just happen to be in the wrong place at the wrong time. What's more frightening is that often everything a thief needs to commit identity theft is located in that wallet or purse—driver's license, credit cards, and surprisingly enough, often social security cards. It's important for people to realize that low tech doesn't mean less effective.

So first let me start by saying that if you have your social security card in your wallet, purse, glove compartment of your car, or anywhere else other than a secured location in your home, go retrieve it right now and lock it away safely in your home. With that out of the way, we have already greatly reduced your risk of identity theft when it comes to pickpockets. However, though it has been changed now in every state, there are still thousands of older driver's

> It's important for people to realize that low tech doesn't mean less effective.

licenses out there that contain social security numbers. In addition, even without the social security number, just getting the driver's license is a great start to obtaining the info needed for identity theft.

I have to admit that I have always been fascinated by street performers who dazzle crowds with magic and embarrass them with the same skills employed by the better pickpockets. The woman who stands there talking with the street performer is convinced that she is about to see a cigarette stuck right through the middle of a quarter. Amazing. But as she starts to walk away, the street vendor calls back to ask for the time. As the woman looks down at her arm, the street vendor shows the rest of the crowd the woman's watch he pilfered right off her wrist.

Pickpockets use the same techniques as the street performers; only they don't plan to let the victim in on their little prank. Easy targets, large crowds, and colorful distractions are all part of the pickpocket's arsenal. I once traveled with a coworker and noticed that, instead of carrying a wallet, he placed his ID and credit cards in his backpack.

I asked him about it, and he explained that it was more secure to keep everything in the backpack than having to deal with a wallet while on the road. In theory, it made sense. Of course, when we were standing in line at the airport, he was in front of me wearing his backpack. I simply unzipped the front compartment where he kept his ID and took it out. I then zipped it back up and waited.

As we got closer to the guy who was checking IDs to allow us to board our flight, my friend began to search for his ID. A complete look of panic struck as he realized that it was gone. Of course, knowing the kind of person I am, it didn't take him long to start pointing fingers, and I eventually confessed. Keep in mind I am no professional pickpocket. The simple fact is that he had no clue what was going on behind him, and anyone could have opened up that backpack. He kept his ID and credit cards in his front pants pocket the rest of the trip.

Baggy pants, large jackets, fanny packs, and open purses are all easy targets for the average pickpocket. If you are in an area that is crowded, a simple bump from a person passing by might go unnoticed. That simple bump is often all it takes to separate you from your valuables. By now, everyone has heard the story of the woman who left her purse in the grocery cart while she shopped. She turned her head for just one minute, and her purse was gone. I find that every time I am at the grocery store, I can't help but look to see if there is a purse left unattended. More times than not, there is one that I could easily steal were I to be a thief.

I once read a story about a pickpocket who used to post signs in the subway that would say beware of pickpockets. He would then sit there and watch people as they walked by. As people read the sign, almost unconsciously they would reach for their wallet to make sure it was still there. The pickpocket would take note of where the wallet was, and if the person looked like an easy target, he would simply follow his mark for another five minutes, and then he would steal the victim's wallet. It seems so simple, yet that's the whole point.

In some cases, the pickpocket works with an accomplice. In these cases, it's all about the distraction. One man trips and falls in front of you, dropping papers everywhere. You stop to help, along with a couple other people. While your mind is on helping the man, his accomplice is focused on you. In other cases, there might be a drunk

31

who is shouting obscenities, a woman who is asking for directions, and sadly enough even children are used to keep your attention.

The trick to keeping your valuables safe is following some simple rules.

- If you're wearing baggy pants, keep your wallet in your front pocket. Your wallet's by no means safe from a pickpocket, but it makes stealing it a little more difficult.

- When in a crowded area such as a subway, concert, street fair, sporting event, remain alert. Know where your valuables are, and if you are being continually bumped, keep your hand over your wallet or your purse held tight across your chest.

- If you have zippers, buttons, or snaps, use them. Again, they're not going to stop a pickpocket, but they may slow one down just enough.

- Wearing a coat or jacket with an inside pocket provides a far better place to store a wallet or valuables than any external pocket.

- Don't carry credit cards you don't plan on using. Most people use only one credit card. If that's the case, carry only that one.

- Keep track of your credit cards. Make a list that you keep at home of every credit card you have and the 800 number to report a lost or stolen card. This way, if your wallet or purse is stolen, you can immediately call and cancel the cards that have been put at risk.

- File a police report. No, your wallet will probably not be found, but in the future if your identity is stolen, this report will help you in your efforts to clean everything up.

TRUTH

9

Home burglaries and identity theft

When your home is robbed, it's a traumatic time. You feel violated and begin to play the "what's missing" game. Often, people do not realize everything that was stolen until months or even years later. I remember the first time our house was robbed. I was about 6 years old, and the burglars came in through my sister's window. They ended up getting away with a few items of value, but it is safe to say they were not going to be living life high on the hog after that heist. Well, that theft was a long time ago, and through the years, both security systems and criminals have changed.

Today's burglar has learned from the mistakes of the past. Today's burglar is after more than your television, your DVD player, or your fine silverware. While in theory it's great to steal a plasma TV, the logistics of unbolting it from the wall, being inconspicuous while carrying it out of the house, and having a big enough vehicle to haul the sucker away in a hurry make for a difficult process. Then you have to find a place to pawn it while running the risk of getting caught. While you may ultimately end up making a few hundred bucks, the amount of work you just put in is more than if you had just served fries at McDonald's for a few days. But what if there were something that you could steal that was small enough to stick in your pocket, worth more than all the items in the house combined, and was extremely difficult for authorities to track down? Turns out the high-tech burglar is doing just that.

> Today's burglar has learned from the mistakes of the past.

Recently, I was doing a segment for a TV show in which I had hoped to stage a home break-in to demonstrate the kind of job today's burglar might pull off. Unfortunately, between the lawyers and the insurance companies, that segment was never aired. However, I can still share what we did and what we had planned to do.

The break-in

For this test, a pair of my friends agreed to let me rob their home. All they were told is that I would break in and rob their home. They were not told what I would be looking for, when I would do it, or what my ultimate goal was. Of course, I guaranteed that anything that I "borrowed" would eventually be returned.

Just a few days later, I was in their kitchen going through each of the counter drawers. I guessed I had at least an hour available since they had left only minutes before heading out to what I assumed would be dinner. I was trying to locate their bills and other documents. Most people keep some level of paperwork either in or near the kitchen, and it seemed like just a good a place to start as any.

After just a couple minutes in the kitchen and not finding what I needed, I moved from room to room opening every closet door and going through every box I could find. My goal? I was on a hunt for social security numbers. I was pleasantly surprised when I came upon a box labeled "tax returns," which was stored on an overhead shelf in one of the closets. Inside was the jackpot: I found complete information including their names, address, social security numbers, and even their employment information, including salary. I had everything I would need to continue my master plan.

I snapped off a few photos using my camera phone and put the items back in the box. Since I found that box within 15 minutes of entering the house, I figured I had time to continue to poke around. In their home office, I found an envelope from the DMV that contained driver's license renewal information, meaning I had their driver's license numbers. Another camera phone picture, and I was back to searching. Also discovered during my search were both of their birth certificates, which I took. After about 45 minutes, I tidied up a little and left. The only sign I had been there was the screen missing from the window in the bathroom and a small stuffed dog that I moved from its perch on the couch to its new location on the front porch.

When they returned home and saw the stuffed dog on the porch, they assumed I had been there and decided to call me to find out what I had done. I explained that I had burglarized their home per our agreement. They said they had looked around and didn't think anything was missing. Of course, nothing of note was missing, but they had just been robbed. Were I an identity thief, I would have just gained enough information to obtain a new driver's license under their names, get an apartment, open new credit cards, purchase a car, get a job, and even get arrested—all under their identities. Of course, had this been a real burglary, the homeowners would have been left to assume that the would-be thief must have been scared off before he could actually steal anything. They would continue their lives without the slightest suspicion of the bad credit that was awaiting them in the near future.

Safeguarding confidential documents at home

People never think they will be the victim of a home burglary, yet the FBI reports that a home in the United States is broken into every 14 seconds. This means that while you have been reading this Truth, five homes have been burglarized. While taking proactive steps to protect your home from a burglary is important, it is just as important that you are taking the steps necessary in the event that your home is burglarized.

- Anything that contains your social security number, driver's license number, or other financial account numbers should be kept in a secure place such as a safety deposit box at the bank or a small safe. If you don't have access to either of these, you can hide the documents in a mislabeled box such as baby pictures or kids poems. But I recommend shredding any documents that contain confidential information unless they are absolutely critical to keep.

- As for documents that you must store, simply removing or scratching out the confidential numbers is a great way to prevent the information from falling into the wrong hands.

- In the event that your home is broken into, immediately cancel all your credit cards, and notify your financial institution of a possible security risk to your account. In addition, contact one of the big three credit reporting agencies, and have it put a security lock on your social security number. This prevents an identity thief from opening any new credit on your account.

TRUTH

10

Walk right in and steal whatever you like

I doubt it would come as much of a surprise that it is hard for me to go anywhere without paying attention to potential security flaws. For example, when I go to hotels, I can't help but pay attention to the person being checked in before me. I always end up knowing their name, room number, and what their luggage looks like. On more than one occasion, I have been traveling with coworkers and, using the information I gathered during their check-in, I have been able to commit one type of identity theft and impersonate that person to gain access to their room. Were I a real criminal, I could have stolen their laptop and any other valuables they may have left in their rooms. Being me, I simply steal all their toilet paper and pillows which, depending on the situation, could end up being even worse, I suppose.

The point is that when people think of identity theft, they generally think of the technical attacks via computers and credit cards. However, flaws in physical security can be just as devastating.

I was once hired to test the security of a health-care facility. While management had assigned me to attempt to gain access to the clients' confidential records, they had assumed that my focus would be on hacking into its network via the Internet. Instead, I scheduled an appointment to be seen by a physician.

When I was escorted back to the exam room, I passed several other exam rooms, most of which had the doors closed, with folders tucked into plastic trays hanging on the outside of each room. The nurse escorting me to my room placed a similar folder in the tray on the door to the room I was in, and then she left. The folder contained my medical records, which the office kept on file. After the doctor eventually examined me, he left me to gather my things and exit to the front desk unescorted.

> When people think of identity theft, they generally think of the technical attacks via computers and credit cards. However, flaws in physical security can be just as devastating.

When I exited the room, I noticed that no one was paying attention to me. So instead of heading toward the door, I went the opposite direction. As I passed by the additional exam rooms, I took each folder on the door and placed it into the briefcase that I had carried in with me. I then turned around and headed back toward the exit, taking any additional folders on the doors that I had not yet passed. Just before I got to the exit, I noticed a room with the door open just to the right of the exit. I walked inside what appeared to be a records room and found a wall rack that contained hundreds more folders. I grabbed a handful and stuck them in my case.

I exited the records room, and as I came out, I almost walked directly into the woman who had originally escorted me back to the exam room. She looked stunned to see me coming out of the records room. I smiled and asked where the exit was, and she kindly pointed me in the right direction. As I walked out the door of the facility, I called my primary contact for that company from my cell phone and had him immediately come take the confidential folders back into the facility. I ended up with 27 folders, each containing the confidential information of a patient. While 27 might not seem like a big deal, I could have been in business for quite some time if I were a real identity thief.

One reason that I have found physical security often fails is that the organization grows too quickly. Many times, the original plan of the facility was designed with security in mind. Customers have access to the public areas, while employees are situated in private areas where they can keep potentially confidential information safe. Then the company outgrows its space, 20 new employees are hired, and suddenly cubes are going up where a reception area used to be. Now the restrooms used by the public are located right next to these cubes, and the separation of public and private areas falls apart.

Another security mistake is the placement of printers in a facility. I have lost count of the number of times I have been at a location under the guise of being a customer, and as I walked down a hall, I passed by a printer with documents still sitting on it. In other cases, there have been small boxes next to the printer where people have placed orphaned items that no one has claimed. The crazy thing is that often these documents contain confidential customer information. I simply grab everything I can, throw it into my case, and continue walking. With this type of theft, no one is any wiser, because when the employees go to the printer and the page is not there, they simply assume it failed to print and print it again.

While the challenge of physical security never ends, here are a few simple tips to help improve the security at your office.

■ Do not place a fax machine or printer in an area where the general public can have easy access. If the public walks the same halls as the employees, place the printer in a closed room or in a cubicle off the main walking areas. If I can't see it while I am walking down a hallway, I won't be visiting it.

■ If cubicles must be placed near heavy foot-traffic areas, choose the employees who occupy these cubes wisely. Make sure that people occupying those cubes either don't have access to confidential company materials or don't leave sensitive materials lying out in the open where passersbys can see them.

■ In some offices, customers may be required to wait in a common area. Be certain that while they are in this area, they are not able to view any employee's computer monitor. From time to time, I visit a site that has the customer service desks out with the public. While I am waiting for the next available person, I can watch employees' monitors as they type in confidential information.

■ Don't allow hitchhikers. While most secured facilities already have "hitchhiker" rules, it is rare they are actually followed. A *hitchhiker* is a person who walks through a secured door on the heels of another person, allowing the person with the proper credentials to give him access. While difficult, enforcement of the no hitchhiker rule is mandatory to the physical security of a facility.

■ Log off computers when you are away from your desk. The idea that you will only be gone for a minute is a major mistake. If I can gain physical access to a logged-in computer for even 30 seconds, I can load malicious software that allows remote access at a later time. Auto-locking screen savers that engage after 2 minutes of nonuse are a good way to lock down employee computers.

■ Don't leave confidential information where anyone can access it. Walk through your facility pretending to be a thief. Anything that *you* can steal is easy pickings for an accomplished thief.

TRUTH

11

Social engineering tactics

People often ask me how hard it is to hack a password. In reality, it is rare that I ever need to hack someone's password. Though there are numerous ways to gain passwords on a network and hundreds, if not thousands, of tools available to crack encrypted passwords, in the end I have found that it is far easier to simply ask for them.

A perfect example of this type of attack was a medium-sized bank that I was testing recently. The bank's concern was related to the new virtual private network (VPN) capabilities it had rolled out to a number of its staff. The VPN allowed staff to connect directly to their secured network while at home or on the road. There is no doubt that a VPN can increase productivity, but there are some pretty major risks that can come with that convenience. The bank explained that the VPN was tied into its Active Directory server. For people who are not technical, basically this just means that when employees log in via the VPN, they use the same credentials they use to log on to their computer at the office.

So I went back to my office, sat down, and picked up the phone. The first call I made was to find out the name of an employee in the IT department. I called the company's main line to the bank, pressed 0, and asked to speak with someone in the IT department. I was asked what I was calling about, so I told the employee I was receiving emails from that bank that seemed malicious. I could have used a number of excuses, but I have found that if you tie in an unhappy customer with a potential security issue, your call gets further up the food chain. In this case, I reached a man who I will call Bill Smith. I made up a story about the email, and after a few minutes, he was able to explain to me that I had called the wrong bank and it was actually another bank's email address that it was coming from. I thanked him for his help and hung up. Obviously, the email address I told him was different, because I didn't want any red flags to continue at the bank's office, and I wanted the call to end quickly.

That night I called the main office number and got the voice mail system. After browsing around for a while, I had gathered a number of names and extensions for employees throughout the organization. The next morning I was ready for action.

I called an employee at the company from the list I had obtained the night before and identified myself as Bill Smith from the IT department. My caller ID was spoofed (easily done with publicly available tools), so it appeared as though I were calling from an internal line. I explained to the employee that I was calling to see if she had any troubles logging into the system, adding that it appeared on my end that she was having login issues. She agreed to log off and log back in while we were talking. I told her that I wasn't seeing her account and asked for her username and password so that I could log in to her account on my end to check the problem. She gave them to me. I ultimately had access to the VPN—without raising any suspicion about my real identity or purpose.

And just like that, the call was over, and I had a username and password that was allowed VPN access into the network. Now, you might be thinking to yourself that you would never be so foolish as to fall for such as obvious attack, and maybe you're right. But generally I can get a pretty good read on a person as the call goes on and hang up long before I ever ask for the password, if I think that person may be on to me. Then I just move on to the next employee. You might also believe that these employees probably know each other and wonder how could I trick them. It's generally rare that the IT staff hang out with people in other departments. So odds are in my favor. Once I worked with a guy named Jake who was making one of these calls. About halfway through, the woman he was talking to stopped and asked, "Is this really Tommy?" Without missing a beat, Jake said, "Of course, it is, baby. You going out on a date tonight with me or what?" It was a gamble on his part, but it worked perfectly. She responded with, "Tommy, you are too funny!" The thing is, when you're an identity thief on the phone, you really have nothing to lose, so you can just go for it and see what happens.

Once I had the VPN access and was on the bank's network, it took me no time at all to gain access to the banking application. From there, I was able to pull up the accounts of every one of the bank's customers. This included names, account numbers, social security numbers—basically everything an identity thief would need.

Each time I have performed this type of attack and then later spoken with the employees who unwittingly gave me the keys to the kingdom, they have all said almost the same thing: They have been told to never give their password to anyone, but that the IT guy is the one who controls all that stuff, so they just assumed that if he wanted it, it was okay. Besides, the IT guy was the one who made their account, and he could change it if he wanted. When asked if they had ever considered that someone might impersonate the IT guy who they blindly trust, they generally said they just never thought it would happen.

The problem now is that you end up with the same advice that the employee had already been given. Never give out your password to anyone. The best advice that I can give is to relay this story, explain it to all employees, or take note of it yourself. If someone from IT, your manager, the CEO of the company, or the president of the United States calls you and at any point in time asks for your password, the answer should always be the same. Do not give out your password to anyone—I mean anyone—no matter how much that person pushes or how convincing, charming, or funny he may be. The answer should simply be "no."

Do not give out your password to anyone.

TRUTH

12

Wolves in sheep's clothing

The first time I ever broke into a bank, I will admit I was nervous. I had no idea what I was doing and was convinced that I would be caught and arrested. Fortunately for me that didn't happen, and more than 1,000 robberies later, I am still able to say that I have never been caught. Of course, by now, you have no doubt surmised that I have been hired by these banking institutions to test the security of their facilities. From banks to law firms, government facilities to biotech companies, my job has been to get in, gain access to confidential information, and get out without being detected. While I have never taken a penny, the information that I have been able to acquire would have been worth billions to an identity thief.

The type of attack that I use to perform these tests is known as social engineering, which is when you use deception to gain access to a desired objective. In my case, I use it to gain access to confidential information generally stored in what is assumed to be a secured facility. While many facilities don't have armed guards, they still have a level of security that is expected to stop the average person from simply walking in, taking what he wants, and walking away. But that is exactly what I do.

Throughout the years, I have worn numerous costumes including pest inspector, air-conditioning repairman, OSHA inspector, fire inspector, phone repairman, flower delivery guy, and local reporter. Basically, I become whatever person it takes to get into whatever location I was hired to infiltrate.

> They still have a level of security that is expected to stop the average person from simply walking in, taking what he wants, and walking away. But that is exactly what I do.

First you need to get an appointment scheduled. I have found that sending email on behalf of one employee to another employee is the fastest way to achieve this. For example, if my character of the day is going to be in pest control, someone from my office will call the target location and ask who she should speak to about contracting pest control services.

Often the employee gives the name of the facility manager. Using that information, I send a spoofed email from the facility manager to office managers at different locations explaining that we have hired XYZ Pest Control to come in and check for bugs. *Spoofing*, or forging email on behalf of someone else, is extremely easy to do and often a quick way to get an appointment on the books. These emails always work.

Whenever possible, I try to go to the company I am infiltrating with a partner. I find that it gives us far more opportunity to split up and cover more ground unaccompanied, which is probably the most important part of the whole attack and where most organizations fail to enforce their policies.

When I arrive at the location as a pest inspector, I carry in my tool bag. While it does contain some pest control materials, it also holds tools of thief's trade, such as a wireless access device and CDs containing software that allows me to control that computer later from a remote location. If my partner and I are able to wander through the facility unaccompanied, we begin to look for places that we can plug our wireless device into the company's network. The hope is to place it where it will not be noticed. If we are successful, we now have access to the bank's internal network from our car in the parking lot of the facility.

Additionally, we are looking for computers that have been left logged in while people are away from their desks. When we find one, we drop one of our CDs into that computer. The CD contains a communication terminal application, which instructs that computer to begin talking with a system back at our main headquarters. From that point on, we are able to give the computer any instruction we like from a computer at our headquarters, and it will be executed as though the employee using that computer ran it.

While gaining access to the network is definitely important when infiltrating an organization, simply picking up what we have been hired to steal and walking out with it is sometimes much faster. Many organizations back up their databases on a daily basis. Those backup tapes often end up on shelves in the server room neatly labeled for all to see. Backup tapes are not the only thing I take. Laptops, PDAs, any interesting documents, keys, CDs, and pretty much anything that may contain confidential information go right into my bag.

There are some instances in which an employee makes an attempt to escort me while I am performing an "inspection." In those cases, I do everything in my power to shake them. I ask for a cup of coffee, send the employee to get me a pen, or ask for needed documentation. If I get really desperate, I simply tell the person I am not feeling well and then head to the restroom. After about 15 minutes, I come out and find that my escort has left. I have yet to find someone who is that dedicated to the escort policy.

Following are some suggestions for tightening security at your business.

- Always escort visitors while they are in nonpublic or secured areas. Most organizations already have policies requiring visitors to be escorted, but I find that it is rarely properly enforced. In my opinion, this policy should be grounds for immediate termination if an employee fails to follow it.

- Don't trust email. When an email comes from one employee instructing another employee to release information, give access, or load software, the email should always be validated with a phone call. It takes 30 seconds to confirm the validity of the email. Without it, you have no idea if the email is legitimate or just me getting ready to "visit" your facility.

- Ask visitors to show a valid driver's license before you give them access to private or secured areas. Though there is no guarantee the driver's license is real, just getting that information will make that person far less likely to take chances.

- Make sure your surveillance cameras are obvious. No one wants to be on camera stealing something. Just seeing the cameras is often enough of a deterrent. Don't have cameras? Put up fake ones. A potential identity thief is not going to know the difference.

- Train your employees. Many people have no idea that there are people like me who will just walk in and steal things while everyone else is working around them. After I have robbed a company, I train the employees on how to avoid future attacks. Later, I often send a second team to test them again and find that it's rare we have the same success.

TRUTH

13

No respect for their elders

It should be clear by now that a social security number (SSN) is the key to your information security. From health care to car purchases, your SSN is what makes you who you are—at least in the eyes of the government, banking institutions, credit card companies, and the like. But often forgotten is the whole point of the SSN.

If you are old enough, you probably remember the plan for every American over the age of 64 to be guaranteed a secure retirement. Well, the age has been changed to 67, and by the time I'm old enough to collect, all the baby boomers will have drained the system dry. But for now, it's working as planned. Each month, my parents collect their social security check and spend it on lawn gnomes and bad sweaters.

Unfortunately, there are some who feel that the retired are already living the good life and might be better off penniless and confused. Just when you think they couldn't sink any lower, identity thieves make prime targets out of the elderly, who often can barely survive through their social security checks.

Identity thieves often seek out the elderly for a number of reasons.

- The elderly often live alone and have fewer family members and friends looking out for them every day. This can often isolate them and make them a primary target to a thief.

- They are also less likely to realize they have become a victim and, if they do discover it, they are less likely to report the crime.

- The elderly tend to be far more trusting and in many cases lonely, which gives the benefit of the doubt to strangers who are kind to them.

- Elderly people often have a large amount of disposable income and an excellent credit rating.

Whether or not all of these stereotypes are true, the point is that people who are 70 years or older are primary targets of identity thieves.

In a common ruse, identity thieves call an elderly person claiming to be performing a survey. The survey might be on anything from television shows to the types of food the victim eats. While many younger people simply explain they do not have the time to waste on such calls, often the elderly are happy to give their opinions. During the call, the thief attempts to strike up conversations outside of the "survey" questions. This allows them to gain more and more personal information under the guise that they are simply enjoying talking with the victim.

Thieves will attempt to harvest personal Information, such as

■ Name and home address

■ Primary physician's name

■ Insurance provider

■ Names of relatives and what towns they live in

■ Do you live alone?

■ Do you receive a pension?

■ Do you have any pets? What are their names?

■ Do you own your home? How long have you lived there?

■ Do you own a car? What kind is it?

While most of these questions may seem benign in nature, all of the information gathered can be used later by the skilled identity thief. Upon completion of "the survey," the thief may even go so far as to explain how much he enjoyed the call and ask if he can call again another time just to talk more. Establishing a relationship with the victim often opens the door to long-term compromise.

Starting with those earlier questions, the identity thief has many options for performing his attack. In some cases, he simply waits a week or two and then calls back, this time pretending to be from the insurance company. During the second call, the thief might explain that he is following up on a medical claim that the victim made several months earlier. The thief uses the victim's name and explains that the claim relates back to the victim's physician. Since the thief is initially giving information and not asking for any information, he immediately has credibility with the victim. The thief then tells the victim he has been overpaid and has been attempting to send the victim a reimbursement check. However, the address that the insurance has on record must be incorrect since the check was returned in the mail.

As the thief reads the address back to the victim, he intentionally reverses part of the street number. The victim spots the error and points it out. The thief thanks the victim and then explains for security purposes that he needs to make sure he has truly been talking to the victim and not someone just pretending to be the victim. To do this, the thief needs the victim to verify his SSN. Of course, by now the victim is 100% convinced that this truly is the insurance company and gives the number without a second thought. In some cases, the thief also offers to do a direct deposit if the victim would like. Since often the elderly have a hard time getting out, this is a great service. The victim simply needs to supply his bank account number, and the money will be deposited within 24 hours.

While I have some basic suggestions to prevent the elderly from becoming identity theft victims, often it takes other family members and friends to protect those who are most vulnerable.

- Never agree to take phone surveys or carry on conversations with people you do not know, whether on the phone or in person.

- If you receive a call from someone claiming to be with a government agency or other trusted entity, do not give the caller any personal information. Ask for a case number and contact name, and then call directory assistance to obtain the phone number for the agency and call the person back.

- Sometimes the elderly get into a position where they can no longer manage their finances on their own. This is when a trusted family member needs to step in and help. If there are no family members available, contact the AARP for guidance.

- Never make purchases when a telemarketer calls, when you get an email, or when a salesperson comes to the door.

- If you are taking care of an elderly person, visit often, check the relative's mail, and ask questions. Does the mail contain large amounts of promotional items? If so, your relative may be making questionable purchases and ending up on "suckers" mailing lists. Has your relative made friends with people on the phone? If so, get involved quickly to find out more.

14

Are you paying the IRS or an identity thief?

For many of us in the United States, there is no day more dreaded than April 15. Uncle Sam comes knocking, and we all starting hunting for ways to hide the money we worked so hard to earn. Of course, not everyone is running from the IRS. There are those who actually end up being owed money and look forward to filing for their tax refund. No matter what your situation, everyone faces this form of identity theft, and unlike just about every other Truth I discuss in this book, there is almost nothing you can do about it.

Why am I being audited?

You go online and find a site that claims to allow you to file your tax returns at no charge. The site is part of the IRS e-file program, which the Internal Revenue Service created to allow third-party vendors to file free and pay tax returns. The e-file program is real and does allow people who make less than $54,000 a year to file for free. It seems like a great deal and takes only a few minutes for you to fill out the online form, and just like that your tax return has been filed. If you are expecting a refund, you can also include your bank account number, allowing the IRS to directly deposit the funds right into your account.

While there are a number of these e-file Web sites that are legitimate, there are far more that are only there to commit identity theft. What's worse is that you may not find out until the IRS comes looking for its money that the site you "filed" through was a scam. You see, when you submit your information to the fake site, it doesn't just steal it; it actually turns around and files the return on your behalf to the IRS. The only difference is that these fake sites often change the filing to make sure that you are guaranteed to receive a generous refund, even if it's far more than what you were legally owed.

Why would these fake sites try to get you more money? Because, of course, they have no intention of filing for the funds to be deposited into *your* bank account. Instead, they have the funds diverted to an account that they have set up for the attack. Now, just to add insult to injury, the IRS eventually smells a rat and comes knocking on your door. You're responsible not only to pay back whatever the difference was in the refund, but also any interest that has compiled on that amount. In addition, you can expect the full rubber-glove treatment from the IRS and the audit it will be performing on you.

In other situations, the identity thief running the fake filing site doesn't file at all. Instead, the thief is only interested in gaining all your confidential information to be used for other identity theft attacks. So while you are left to think your taxes have been paid and Uncle Sam is off your back for another year, in reality you're now being sought for tax evasion *and* your identity has been compromised.

Again, expect big fines and more rubber-glove treatment. What's most aggravating about these attacks is that not only are your taxes now a mess, but you will also be dealing with the destroyed credit that has been caused by the identity thief. By now, the thief has probably run up thousands of dollars of credit debt under your name.

So at this point you are probably thinking, "Note to self, don't file online." Well, of course, it's not quite that simple. First, if you want to know who you can trust online, the IRS has set up a Web page of its trusted e-file vendors (www.irs.gov/efile/lists/0,,id=101223,00. html). The problem is that not all identity thieves are up to the task of making big complex Web sites and then waiting around like a spider for a fly in the hopes that you will happen to choose their fake company. Instead, they simply find other ways to gain access to your social security number (SSN), possibly using one of the many attacks listed in this book. Then they simply file on your behalf with a completely fictional tax return. Their goal, of course, is to file early and arrange the numbers for a hefty refund.

Though this type of attack has been around for a number of years, it started to get noticed in 2004 when the IRS noted a 1,000% increase in the number of fake filings between 1999 and 2003. And though the IRS continues to attempt to find ways to prevent these fake filings from happening, to date there has been no solution, and they continue to flood the IRS. In the meantime, my only recommendation is to file as early as you possibly can. If you file first, you win.

When the IRS isn't the bad guy

In January 2008, hundreds of thousands of confused and concerned people received an email purportedly from the IRS claiming that they would be audited on their tax return this year. The recipient was instructed to follow a link to a Web site where they were to submit personal information to aid in the audit process.

Of course, the IRS would never send out an unsolicited tax-related email; this was simply another identity theft attack. In fact, the IRS has been faced with so many attacks against taxpayers that it has dedicated an entire area of its Web site to phishing and ID theft-related matters (www.irs.gov/newsroom/article/0,,id=155682,00.html).

Of course, not all tax-related identity theft attacks happen on the Internet. In fact, some of the more successful types of attacks have taken place over the phone. In 2008, the IRS had to deal with yet another situation in which imposters began a calling campaign. When the victim answered the phone, the caller explained he was with the IRS and that he had recently sent a refund check from the IRS to the victim. However, according to IRS records, the check had still not cleared, so the IRS had flagged the check as having been lost. The caller asks for the victim to instead give a bank account number where he would like the funds deposited, and the IRS will use direct deposit to transfer the funds.

Guess what? The IRS doesn't care if you've cashed a refund check and would probably be grateful if you never did. If you ever receive a phone call from anyone claiming to be with the IRS or any other government service, it's best to keep your confidential information confidential. Much like Big Brother, anyone calling you regarding real issues will already have every piece of information about you on file. There will never be a case where legitimate people will be asking you for your information.

TRUTH

15

What do you mean there's a warrant out for my arrest?

It's late in the afternoon, and you're sitting back watching the game. Suddenly your dog starts barking, and then you hear a knock at the door. You start to prepare yourself to dismiss whatever salesperson has decided to interrupt your game. You open the door, but instead of seeing kids selling candy or the creepy guy selling magazine subscriptions, there is a police officer. In fact, there are two of them, and one is holding a pair of handcuffs.

This is definitely not the way you expected this day to go. One of the officers states your name and asks if it's you. You nod, and immediately the officers begin to place you into handcuffs. As your kids and neighbors look on, you only pick up parts of what is happening. Did they just say, "outstanding warrant?" You ask them to tell you what they are talking about, but they just continue handcuffing, searching, and placing you into a squad car. Five minutes ago, you were relaxing at home. Now you're in the backseat of a squad car heading to jail. What the hell just happened?

When you get to the station, everything is made clear. According to the police, you were arrested for stealing a car and let out on bail a year ago. When you didn't appear at your trial date, a warrant was issued for your arrest. Well, that makes much more sense, except that you never stole a car, were never arrested, and have never posted bail. You explain all that to the officers, and in time, they will get it straightened out. In the meantime, however, you have just become a victim of criminal identity theft.

Five minutes ago, you were relaxing at home. Now you're in the backseat of a squad car heading to jail. What the hell just happened?

Later, after mug shots and fingerprints are compared, the police do determine that you aren't the person who committed these crimes; rather, someone committed these crimes while impersonating you. The officers release you. However, that does not mean your record has been cleared. In fact, there are no established procedures for clearing your criminal record, and it is up to you to push to get the matter resolved.

In addition, your record being tarnished can have other far-reaching effects. For instance, a short time after this whole ugly incident, say you just found the perfect job, and they love you. All you have to do is pass the background check, and you are home free. The only problem is that you have an outstanding warrant on your record. Good luck convincing the potential employer that it's all just a big mistake and they should hire you anyway.

Cases of criminal identity theft have popped up all over the world. Most often the criminal has illegally obtained a driver's license using your personal information. When the thief is arrested, he uses your name, SSN, and driver's license as his identification. Once the thief, posing as you, is let out on bail, he disappears, becoming someone new while the real you still exists and can be tracked down. What's more, you might have no idea there is a warrant out for your arrest until years later when you are pulled over for a routine traffic stop.

Once you become aware that you are victim of this type of attack, you need to immediately take action to resolve this issue. Though there is no one right way to get this resolved, the steps that follow will at least get you headed in the right direction.

1. Get out of jail. The comparison of mug shots and fingerprints can generally solve identity disputes. In the case where these items were not obtained, you have to rely on signature comparisons, alibis, and other information that can be used to prove you were not where the crime took place at the time it occurred.

Once the thief, posing as you, is let out on bail, he disappears, becoming someone new while the real you still exists and can be tracked down.

2. Contact the arresting agency. You need to make sure the arresting agency understands that you are not the person it arrested, prove your identity, and then have the agency file an impersonation report. Once the report is completed, you need that agency to recall any warrants it has issued in your name and supply you with documentation that indicates that you are

59

cleared of this crime. That documentation is your get out of jail free card; you should carry that with you until this entire matter has been resolved.

3. Once you have proven you are not that person who committed the crime in question, request that your name be removed from the criminal records. Often, the arresting agency will not know who the real person was, but it can place a "John Doe" in the file instead of your name. Be aware that your name will still be kept in the file as an alias.

4. Eventually, you are probably going to need to deal with the courts. Though you can attempt to do this on your own, I strongly recommend that you bring in a criminal defense attorney. Your attorney will understand the laws in your state and exactly what will be needed to completely clear your name not only from the local and state records, but also in the FBI files.

5. Don't forget about the DMV. In many states, you have the right to have a new driver's license number issued if you can prove that someone is using your existing driver's license number. Of course, obtaining that proof requires following a number of the preceding steps first. In the meantime, you can contact the DMV and ask to have your license flagged for potential fraud.

6. Some states have set up specific programs to deal directly with criminal identity theft. For example, California has set up a criminal identity theft registry at www.oispp.ca.gov/consumer_privacy/consumer/documents/pdf/cis8englsih.pdf. This document not only gives terrific information on how to deal with criminal identity theft, but it also allows the victims to be placed on a statewide list that can protect them from future criminal identity theft attacks. It also notifies officers of the existing issues. To find out if your state offers a similar service, contact your local law enforcement agency.

TRUTH

16

Medical identity theft

Through the years, I have made attempts to test every kind of identity theft attack I know of. However, when it comes to medical identity theft, even I had to draw the line. Once again, you are sitting at home going through your bills and notice an envelope from the ACME medical clinic with the words "Payment Due" printed in bold font on the front. You open and read the billing statement, which indicates that you need to pay for the wart removal you had performed six months earlier. The problem is that you have never been to the ACME medical clinic, and you are quite certain you have never had a wart removed. You may not realize it yet, but you have just become the victim of medical identity theft. Worse still is that medical identity theft actually makes your basic run of the mill credit identity theft seem like a walk in the park.

When someone uses your ID to make purchases, you have a number of options to clear the matter up, and most often you will be able to get the charges removed. Even your bad credit can eventually be cleaned up. Medical identity theft, on the other hand, is an entirely different kettle of fish. Even if you can prove that you did not have those services performed, the information that ended up in your medical file is most likely there for life. That's because, while you can have notes added to your file, you cannot force information to be deleted from your file.

In 2005, a study by the Federal Trade Commission (FTC) found that approximately 3% of identity thefts were related to medical identity theft. That translates to about 249,000 victims. Though no official study has been released since then, there is no argument that number has grown significantly with rising health care costs, giving identity thieves all the more reason to commit theft.

When researching medical identity theft, I was astonished to see the stories about victims who found themselves in the uncomfortable position of often being guilty until proven innocent. For example, if you report fraudulent charges to a hospital or doctor's office, you will discover that hospitals and doctor's offices are obliged to protect the identity thief's real identity! That means someone you don't know could steal your identity, wrack up charges in your name, and even if you clear your name of the debt the thief incurred, the medical community cannot release the thief's real identity or expunge the services performed on this other person from your records.

In one case I researched, an Alabama man received a $10,000 bill related to a hand injury he didn't sustain. When he reported the fraudulent claim, the medical institution immediately stopped giving him any information related to the bill. In addition, the institution would not release the medical file to him, yet it continued to press for him to pay for the services. With nowhere else to turn, the man found a television reporter who convinced the hospital to take a new x-ray of the man's hand so the hospital could compare it to the x-ray it had on file. When the x-rays didn't match, the victim was able to prove his innocence.

In another case that shows how the system works against the victim, a woman in Illinois received a $2,000 bill for delivering a baby at a Miami hospital. She explained that she had never been to that hospital and, more importantly, the procedure they were claiming was simply not possible. Thee woman was 72 years old! But the calls continued, and the woman had to spend several weeks going from agency to agency to finally prove that she had not recently given birth.

Dealing with the issues related to collections from a false claim made by a medical identity thief can be trying and take months or even years to resolve. However, there is a much bigger concern that is growing in the medical community. There are those in positions of power who would like to create one master database to hold all our medical records. This would mean that you could visit a hospital or doctor anywhere and have your records pulled up instantly, potentially saving your life. The downside, however, is if you have been the victim of medical identity theft, your records could be mixed with a thief's records, which could endanger your life!

When your identity is stolen, you can file for fraud protection for your credit, but it turns out with medical identity theft, there is no such option in place. In fact, if someone is using your personal information for any medical treatment, you may not find out for years. Then when you do, you have no simple way to stop it. You have no rights to correct bad information that ends up in your medical file, and as I mentioned before, you may no longer be able to even see your own medical file.

You have no rights to correct bad information that ends up in your medical file.

Further, your medical records are used when you apply for health or life insurance (not to mention for some jobs). What if your medical records contain not only your records but also records from someone else who has had a serious illness? You could find yourself blackballed from every insurance agency on the planet. Good luck trying to convince these agencies that the information in your medical report isn't yours.

Because this is not a situation where the thief even needs to have to your SSN to begin the scam, it is up to you to attempt to watch for any potential anomalies when it comes to your medical history.

Unfortunately, there is little advice I can give you other than to be vigilant.

- Your health insurance company generally sends a written response to every claim that is filed by a health care provider. Most often it is just to acknowledge that it has covered the costs. It is important that you read every one of these notices. If you receive a notice and don't know what it is related to, call the insurance company to get more detail. If it's fake, immediately notify your insurance company and begin making calls to the institution that filed the claim.

- If you do find that you have become the victim of medical identity theft, prepare yourself for a long and aggressive fight. These types of attacks do not clean up easily, could go on for years and, if you are not persistent, the identity thief will win.

- Because this type of crime is not well known and you have few resources at your disposal, contacting the U.S. Attorney's office in your state may be the easiest way to find additional help. Contact information can be found at www.usdoj.gov/usao/offices/index.html.

TRUTH

17

Sweet 16 and already a victim!

If you are a parent of a teenager, you already know the risks that the Internet can pose. By now you have probably heard the stories about adult predators who hang out in online chat rooms looking for children to victimize. Often these freaks pose as teenagers, attempting to gain the trust of unsuspecting and naive children. News reporters have posed as potential child victims, agreed to meet with predators, planted hidden cameras, and caught these criminals in compromising positions.

It is obviously extremely important that all parents are aware of these risks to make sure their children know who they should and shouldn't be talking with. However, there is another risk that children are facing online that often parents are completely unaware of. That risk, of course, is identity theft, and it turns out that children can be at even more risk than adults.

I didn't get my first credit card until I was 18 years old. Like most other teenagers, even after I got it, I had no clue what a credit report was, and I was not even slightly interested in reading one. In fact, I didn't find out about credit reports until I bought my first new car a few years later. Had an identity thief been using my information during those years, I would not have known it. And that is exactly why younger people are so much at risk.

The Federal Trade Commission (FTC) has stated that people under the age of 18 are the fastest growing demographic for identity theft. More often than not, young victims won't realize that they are victims until they apply for a driver's license or attempt to sign up for their first credit card. Then, all of a sudden, creditors come out of the woodwork to attempt to recover unpaid debt. In many cases, thieves use portions of the victims' real information while making up the rest. When the victims get credit reports, they find their social security numbers assigned to more than just their names.

So how is it that identity thieves are acquiring these young peoples' SSNs? Well, it turns out that often the victims give it to them while chatting online. While most adults have been made aware of the need to guard SSNs, often teenagers don't have any idea what it's used for or what can happen if it ends up in the wrong hands.

To find out just how difficult, or easy, it would be to convince teen-agers to give out their confidential information, I decided to conduct an experiment. I created a fake company that gave away free MP3 music; something that's attractive to nearly every teen. On the home page, I listed numerous popular bands and explained that the site allowed free and 100% legal downloads. The explanation on the site was that it was only for users under the age of 18. The idea was that the music industry realizes that most young people don't have the money to pay for the music, so instead the site was giving the music away in return for the revenue from advertising that was placed on the site.

As with most attacks, all you need is a story that is remotely plausible and offers something that the potential victim wants. To use this free site, the teens were required to fill out an online form that asked for their full names, addresses, and email addresses. They were also asked to create a login name and password so that they could log in and access all the free downloadable music. In addition, victims were asked to supply their birth dates and SSNs to validate that they were really under the age of 18. The site also told victims that no credit card information was required, as there would be no charge for any of the music. To an unwitting teenager, that sounds quite reasonable and legitimate.

> As with most attacks, all you need is a story that is remotely plausible and offers something that the potential victim wants.

I put the site online and then went hunting. I started by going to the social networking Web sites and creating a user account for a 15-year-old boy. I would attempt to meet as many people as I could and befriend as many people as possible. In addition, I visited blogs, chat rooms, and anywhere else I could find young people to talk to. What was frightening is just how easy it was. Regardless of my intention, it definitely opened up my eyes as to how frighteningly easy it is for predators to be so successful at finding young victims.

My main goal was to get people to go to my fake company and, in all modesty, I think I did a pretty good job of promoting it. In my messages, I posted things about the music I liked and then gave the link to the site, raving about how great it was that a site like it existed. I always mentioned the free music and how it was totally legal. When people would chat with me, I always asked if they had an iPod or if they were into music. If they said no, our friendship ended. If they said "yes," I mentioned a few bands I thought were popular with the kids and then asked if they downloaded their music from my fictitious company. Of course, no one had ever heard of it, so I explained just how cool it was.

Ultimately, I did get people to my site. Over a three-day period, I was able to gather about 25 SSNs.

When I was done with the experiment, I simply changed the site message to say that the company was no longer in business. As for all those who had submitted their information, upon completion of the form, they were informed it would take up to three days to validate their age, and they would receive an email notification when their account had been approved. Of course, it never was.

Had I been a real identity thief, the hour it took to make my fake Web site and a few days of chatting online would have been more than worth it. My youngest victim would have been 14 years old, and my oldest 17.

Had I been a real identity thief, the hour it took to make my fake Web site and a few days of chatting online would have been more than worth it.

Protecting your children's identities

- The best advice I can give to parents of children at any age is to hold on to their social security cards and not give them out until you absolutely have to.

- In addition, if your child comes to you asking for it, ask questions to find out exactly why they need it. Take the time to ensure that it is being used for a legitimate reason.

■ Then, like the conversation about the birds and the bees, sit them down and explain just how complicated and precious their identities really are and that it only takes one time of giving their information to one wrong person for it to haunt them for the rest of their lives.

■ If you are the parent of a child who has had his identity stolen, you should treat this just like you would treat an adult. (See Part IX of this book, "The Truth About Putting a Stop to Identity Theft.") File a police report, notify the reporting agencies, and file for credit freeze and fraud alert. Ultimately, there is no discrimination when it comes to ID theft, and you need to get control as quick as possible.

TRUTH

18

Being dead doesn't protect you from identity theft

In April 2008, federal prosecutors charged a woman in California named Tracy Kirkland (with her 13 aliases) with 15 identity theft–related charges. Her attacks took place between October 2005 and March 2008. What makes this particular identity theft case unique is that all the victims were deceased.

There have been cases in the past in which an identity thief has used the credentials of a deceased individual to create new credit cards, but this was different. You see, Ms. Kirkland found a new way to exploit an old trick already used by many identity thieves.

> What makes this particular identity theft case unique is that all the victims were deceased.

Have you ever called your financial institution and been asked to supply your mother's maiden name to verify who you were? Odds are pretty good that you have. Now try and remember the last time that was the only question the bank asked you. Hopefully you will have to think pretty hard. That's because numerous organizations learned the hard way that tracking down a person's mother's maiden name was not nearly as difficult as they thought.

Go to a Web search engine and type in the word *genealogy*, and you will be shocked to see how many sites are dedicated to helping people create a family tree. In most cases, you are required to set up an account and, while some are free, some sites do charge, though the payoff for an identity thief is worth the investment. Once your account is set up, simply submit any information you have and start searching. Obviously, the more information you have, the more narrow your search becomes. While there are no guarantees that you will find everything you are looking for, tracking down the past is easier than you might think.

As financial institutions started getting burned by identity thieves who were tracking down mother's maiden names, they started requiring additional validation, such as the last four digits of a social security number (SSN), current address, branch location where you set up your account, and so on. Of course, a thief could gather all of this with some time and effort as well, but it has begun to make the process far more difficult for an identity thief to subvert.

Ms. Kirkland took things to a whole new level when she discovered a Web site, Rootsweb.com. The site offers access to the Social Security Administration's death index listing, which is an up-to-date list of people who have passed away, their birthdates, and their SSNs. The Department of Commerce actually publishes this list on a monthly basis to help banks and credit agencies prevent identity thieves from opening new accounts using the names of people who have passed away.

While the idea of this list is logical, Ms. Kirkland realized that she didn't need to go out and create new accounts with this information. Instead, she simply started taking over existing accounts of people who were deceased.

The attack was simple; Ms. Kirkland would go to this Web site and gather the information of deceased individuals, including their names, birthdates, SSNs, and zip codes. She would then use other search engines similar to zabasearch.com to track down the most recent known address for the victims.

Once Ms. Kirkland had gathered as much information as possible about the deceased, she would then start calling every credit card company she could think of. With each call, she would pose as the deceased, verifying if there was an open account with the organization. When she discovered a live account, she would request to put in a change of address. The new address that she provided would go back to one of several mail boxes that she rented.

During the two and a half years that Ms. Kirkland spent committing identity theft, she gained access to over 100 unique credit cards belonging to deceased individuals. This was accomplished because, while the Social Security Administration death index is used to help prevent would-be thieves from creating new credit, many organizations fail to cross-reference this list against their existing customer database on a monthly basis. This means that someone who has passed away could continue to have an open credit account for months or even years after his death.

> Someone who has passed away could continue to have an open credit account for months or even years after his death.

Even if the deceased has friends or family members helping settle his affairs, it's often not possible to accomplish everything quickly, and it is all too easy to miss an account altogether. Of course, this is exactly what Ms. Kirkland spent her time tracking down and exploiting.

The best thing that you can do if you are responsible for putting a person's affairs in order is to request a credit report from each of the three reporting agencies. (See Part IX of this book, "The Truth About Putting a Stop to Identity Theft," for more details.) Then go through them and systematically contact each creditor listed. Doing so should go a long way toward ensuring that you get every account closed.

The following checklist should help to make sure you cover all the basics to prevent the deceased from becoming identity theft victims.

- Notify the post office.

- Review credit reports at least six months after the deceased has passed and make sure no new items have shown up.

- Notify insurance companies (car, medical, home, and so on).

- Notify the landlord if the deceased rented.

- Notify pension providers and life insurance companies.

- Close all bank, credit union, and other financial institution accounts.

- Notify the mortgage provider.

- Notify loan companies.

- Close credit card and store cards.

- Notify utility companies if accounts were in the deceased's name.

- Notify the passport agency and cancel the deceased's passport.

- Notify all additional creditors.

19

Fake credit card applications

Have you ever been accosted from someone looking in one of those little kiosks as you're walking through a mall? The solicitor intercepts you as you walk past, talking you into applying for new cell phone service, signing some whacky petition, or entering a drawing to win a brand new car.

One day I was shopping, and I noticed that people who obviously had no interest in buying a new phone or filling out one of these surveys would actually stop and listen. Next thing they know, they are testing new cell phones, filling out surveys, or signing up with high hopes of winning that brand new car. It was during this time that I had a brilliant idea. I was going to set up a kiosk dedicated to committing identity theft.

> I had a brilliant idea. I was going to set up a kiosk dedicated to committing identity theft.

The plan

My plan was simple. I created a fake credit card company and allowed people to sign up to receive a credit card. I realized there would be a few hurdles I would need to jump through to convince people to give me their confidential information.

First, I needed a company name. So I went online and looked at names of other credit card companies. I made up the name Bankers Card Services, which sounded similar to other names that people may have heard. Next, I had a coworker draw up a few different logos. Once the logo was ready, I created a nice canvas banner that a copy store was more than happy to print for me.

With the company logo set, I now needed a hook. I went with "no interest for the first six months and no annual fees." I then had flyers printed outlining the offer, which added legitimacy to my illegitimate business. I then worked with another engineer to create software that would allow the user to fill out the form using a computer right at the mall. Lastly, I rented a touch screen computer and ordered a professional-looking kiosk. In no time, I was Bankers Card Services and ready to begin stealing identities.

The attack

The first stop was a mall in New Jersey. I set up everything and even purchased several $5 gift cards good for use at the mall. I realized that someone a little younger and a lot prettier might have more success than me at starting successful conversations with strangers. So for this attack, I engaged Jessica, an engineer out of our Baton Rouge office.

Within minutes, Jessica was already succeeding. A friendly couple walking by, stopped, and waited patiently as Jessica told them about no interest for six months and no annual fees. As they talked, she casually walked them over to the kiosk and explained that all they needed to do was apply today to get the $5 gift card. Even if it turned out they didn't qualify, the card was theirs to keep. Not giving the couple a moment to discuss it between themselves, Jessica had the computer screen up and was showing them where to enter their names.

The man typed in his name, address, phone number, social security number (SSN), driver's license number, and mother's maiden name. He clicked the Submit button and, just like that, he was a victim of identity theft. Jessica thanked them, gave him the gift card, handed them a flyer, and told them they would receive a letter in the next couple of weeks letting them know if they qualified for the card. They thanked her and walked away.

Sadly, even I underestimated just how big of a separation there is between an average guy and a pretty girl. Throughout the day, for every person that I pulled in, Jessica pulled in four or five. As we started revealing to people that this entire offer was just an identity theft attack, most had the same response: "She seemed so sweet" or "He seemed like such a nice guy." And that's what makes some identity thieves so successful.

People have an image in their minds of what a criminal should look like. Dark glasses, thick beard, freaky tattoos—you know, the bad guy. No one suspects the cute girl with the long blond hair, bright blue eyes, and sweet southern accent. But the criminal's goal is to be someone you would trust—the girl next door, the guy who bags your groceries, or even someone you might let your kid date.

While the mall turned out to be a huge success, we thought it might be interesting to see how college students might react to this same attack. We packed up and took our credit card offer to Austin, Texas. We set up shop on the sidewalk near the college campus and had the same success. College kids lined up at the chance to get a credit card. Again, when we told them the truth, they also couldn't believe that someone who seemed so nice had actually been lying to them.

Protecting yourself

By now it should be clear that, while many identity theft attacks happen over the phone, via email, or in other ways where the thief can remain anonymous, there are cases in which you will actually meet and shake the thief's hand. You need to be certain you are not making simple and obvious mistakes that could have disastrous results.

- Never give your personal information to anyone unless you are absolutely certain you know who they are and how that information will be used. I realize that sometimes you just can't be totally certain, but it is always better to err on the side of caution.

- Instead of signing up at the kiosk, ask for contact information and do your own research. If you're told the offer is only available while you are there, walk away.

- Just because the people are nice or look innocent doesn't mean you can trust them.

- Even a setup that looks professional or elaborate can be nothing but props to a thief. In reality, it took very little time and money to set up the entire fake business.

- There are probably legitimate businesses that actually offer credit card applications at a mall kiosk or other outdoor locations; my advice is to stay away. If you are looking for a credit card that offers good rates, talk to your friends and see who they use. You can also check with your local banks and credit unions.

TRUTH

20

An identity thief has a gift just for you

You have come home from a long day at the office. As you unlock the door to your house, you notice a small box on the front porch. Inside, you find a letter and a brand new webcam. You didn't order a webcam, so you begin to read the letter. It turns out that the webcam has been sent from a company called Orwell Technology Research Group. The letter explains that they are conducting a study on webcams and their ease of use. All they ask is that you complete a small online survey regarding the installation and setup of your webcam after you install it. As compensation for your time, the webcam is your gift to keep.

A couple days later, you decide to try it out. You plug the webcam into your computer and place the CD into the drive. Less than five minutes later, the camera is installed, and you are waving at your friend online.

So who is Orwell Technology Research Group? I can guarantee it is not a research company dedicated to the betterment of products. In fact, it is a fictional company that I created awhile back for use in identity theft attacks. Were you to visit the Web site that had been listed in that letter, you would have found what appeared to be a professional business. The survey form was real, but all I was interested in was you installing the webcam and software that came with the camera.

The first time I performed this attack, I got a couple engineers together with different skill sets. We purchased a bunch of webcams that cost less than $20 each. We carefully opened the packages and took the webcams out, along with the CD that contained the software. We then took the webcams apart and disabled the little red light that would turn on when the camera was activated. By disabling this light, it guaranteed that the end user would never have any indication of when the camera was on or off.

Next, one of the engineers wrote some new software that would communicate to our network and allow us to access any computer on which it was installed. Of course, the software was designed to be in "stealth" mode so that a user sitting at the computer would not know it was active. Lastly, we made new CDs that contained our new software integrated with the webcam software. The CDs were given new labels, and everything was placed back in the box.

The Orwell Technology Web site we put up was actually just a copy of another organization's real Web site. We simply changed the name and logo and added a survey page. In all, developing the Web site, making the changes to the webcam, creating the new malicious software, and packaging everything took less than three hours.

When the webcam and software were installed, I received notification without the victim's knowledge. At that point, I was able to run commands on the victim's computer via the webcam and the custom software. I could browse the victim's files, take any file I wanted, and read his emails if I so chose. More importantly, I began logging everything the user typed. In other words, if the user was doing online banking, I now had a username and password. If a purchase was being made online, I now had credit card information. But I was able to take it one step further.

> I could browse the victim's files, take any file I wanted, and read his emails if I so chose.

With a command from my computer, I then turned on the webcam that was connected to that computer. This means I truly was "Big Brother" watching. I should probably make it clear that for this test, before I turned the camera on, I did contact the victim, let him know about the attack he had fallen victim to, and asked permission to turn on the camera. While this type of attack falls under the category of creepy, it definitely lends itself to identity theft attacks. In addition, this type of attack can be used by a separated spouse, ex-boyfriend, stalker, or pretty much anyone who wants to pry into your day-to-day life.

Now, you might be thinking to yourself, "I would never have installed that webcam." But what about other software? I have shipped fake AOL CDs, Google software, fake antivirus software, software supposedly from the IRS to help with your taxes, and many other types.

The point is that I can generally find something that a private individual will be willing to load. In fact, I have had just as much success sending it to businesses. All it takes is just one person to load my software onto his computer, and I am in. Generally within minutes, I have access to confidential information. I have even sent out music CDs appearing to be radio station sampler CDs. As soon as the CD is placed into the computer, my malicious software immediately loads. In most cases, this happens without the user's knowledge. In Microsoft Vista, the user gets a warning message, but my software posts a friendly note explaining that it is needed to play the songs. Most users allow the load to continue. Just like the other attacks, once the software is loaded, I have complete access.

I have mentioned many types of attacks that include software being loaded onto your computer. The solution here is simple. Don't install software unless you are absolutely certain you know where it came from and what it will do. Just because it came in a box or has an official letter does not make it any safer. While it's nice to think there are companies sending free gifts and easy-to-use software, in reality it just doesn't usually happen that way.

TRUTH
21

Gift card or gift horse?

When I was growing up, my parents would tell me the old adage, "If it seems too good to be true, it probably is." Generally, these words of wisdom would be offered after I just got done telling them how I was going to make a million dollars by getting involved in one pyramid scheme or another that one of my friends had already fallen for. Of course, my parents were always right, and my friends always lost their money. As I have grown older and hopefully slightly wiser, I find myself using these same words when I speak to others about identity theft. "If it seems too good to be true, it probably is."

The setup

As with many forms of identity theft, it all starts in a seemingly familiar way. You check your mailbox, and among the numerous bills and junk mail, you come across a letter that piques your interest. On the outside, it is labeled "Sweepstakes winner! Prize enclosed!" You open the envelope to find a $50 gift card for a popular home improvement store inside. Included with the gift card is the letter that explains how you won.

> Congratulations!

> [Real store name here] has selected you to win this $50 gift card valid at all [store name] locations. This special gift is yours to keep with no obligation. Over the past 20 years, communities throughout the United States have helped build [store name] into the best do-it-yourself hardware store in the world, and this is our special way of saying thank you to all our valued customers.

> For security purposes, this gift card has not yet been activated. To activate, simply call this toll free number 800-XXX-XXXX and follow the automated attendant.

> We thank you again for your support over the past 20 years and look forward to working with you and your community for years to come.

> Signed...

So you call the 800 number included in the letter. When the line is answered, you hear a woman's prerecorded voice congratulating you again on receiving the free gift card. She then asks that you use the keypad on your phone to input the number located on the gift card below the barcode. You look at the gift card and type the numbers into the phone. When you are done, the automated system responds and spells out your last name and asks you to type 1 if that is your name or 2 if it's not. You press the 1 key. The automated voice now explains that, for security purposes, you need to verify your social security number (SSN) by typing it into the keypad. This is required to verify that the person who is attempting to activate the card is truly the intended recipient. You type in your SSN and, upon completion, the automated attendant congratulates you again, explains that your card is now active, and wishes you a great day.

What happened?

So, what really happened behind the scenes? Well, the first time I performed this attack, I wanted to make sure I made it as convincing as possible. Of course, the home improvement store scam could just as easily be any other well-known store chain. The trick was to make sure whatever I chose would be well received and worth the effort of the recipient to activate it.

The 800 phone number was purchased online and was set to forward to another phone number I had purchased for the attack. The auto attendant I used was simply software I found online and modified for my needs. One of the most important aspects of the attack was the validation of the victim's last name. By spelling this out to the victim, the auto attendant was given a level of legitimacy. In reality, I simply had a database of the cards I was sending out, and I assigned each card to a specific person, so that when the victim typed in the card number, my database had a corresponding last name. For my tests, friends and coworkers let me use their names and addresses. However, a real identity thief could simply buy this type of mailing list online. Hundreds of Web sites sell complete mailing lists including name, address, and in some cases, even household income level.

As for the gift cards, there really was no value to them. In my case, I simply used gift cards that I had already cashed in. Had I been a real identity thief, it would have been just as simple to steal them from the store, as they are not activated until the time of purchase, so they have no value and are not kept secured.

I have heard of other ways of performing this type of attack. In some cases, the letter is from a bank, charity, or research firm. The letter explains that the recipient must take a survey first, and the gift card is provided as a thank-you. Often, the message tells the victim that the IRS considers the gift card to be the same as cash; therefore, the victim's SSN needs to be verified for the gift to be reported. I found that this additional explanation was not needed. This attack can also be done with an online Web site instead of an 800 number. The only difference is that the victim is required to go online to activate the card. No matter what the spin, the ultimate goal remains the same: to get the victim's SSN. Since the identity thief already has the victim's name and address, once he has the SSN, he has everything he needs to become that person.

Of the people who actually took the time to call in, 100% of them gave me their SSN.

I found this type of attack to be very successful and, more importantly, of the people who actually took the time to call in, 100% of them gave me their SSN.

Because this type of attack is so easy to avoid, there is only one major rule that you need to follow. Never give your SSN over the phone. Period. I have yet to find one legitimate reason that any organization should require such information. In some cases they may require the last four digits, but never anything more.

TRUTH

22

That gift card might be worthless

In recent years, gift cards have become the ultimate gift. The people you're buying for get what they want, and you don't have to work too hard at picking out the right gift. Unfortunately, in 2006 and 2007, people in the U.S. started running into a form of theft in which legitimate gift cards purchased in legitimate stores ended up with a zero balance, even though the purchaser had done nothing wrong.

While the person receiving the card was not a victim of having any personal information stolen, the identification of the gift card was being impersonated. What made this more interesting is that this attack was taking place often days before the card was ever purchased.

The original attack is actually quite simple. A thief goes into the store carrying a notepad and a pen. He walks up to the gift card section and grabs a handful of gift cards. As he walks around the store looking as if he is shopping, he nonchalantly writes the gift card numbers on a notepad. The number is generally located on the back of the card just under the printed bar code. Once the thief has written the number down for all the cards, he returns to the wall and hangs the cards back up. The thief then leaves the store without spending a dime.

Most gift cards also contain an available funds verification phone number. This number is provided to allow the owner of the card to call in and get the current balance of the gift card. Beginning that day, the thief starts calling the toll-free number and, when prompted to enter the card number he wants to verify, he submits the numbers he wrote down on his notepad. As he enters each card, the automated attendant responds back that there are no funds available, as expected.

Now, when you activate a card that you plan to give as a gift, the funds suddenly became available. When the thief calls in and supplies the number for that card, instead of having a balance of $0, it now has a balance equal to your generosity. The thief immediately goes online, makes a purchase, submits that gift card number, and has the merchandise shipped to a drop house. By the time you give that gift card to someone else, there is nothing left.

When this scheme first started being reported, corporations realized they needed to do something to protect consumers from these types of attacks. In response, they added an additional security pin to the gift card. The security pin is covered with either a solid sticker or the same silver scratch-off stuff that you might find on a lottery ticket. The idea is that

Since the pin is protected until you reveal the security pin, this guarantees your safety. So you think.

you cannot verify the funds available on the card without submitting both the card number and the security pin. In addition, when attempting to make purchases via the Internet, you are required to submit both the card number and the security pin. Since the pin is protected until you reveal the security pin, this guarantees your safety. So you think.

Unfortunately, that's not exactly true either. The first problem is that most people don't know about the security pin. In fact, when I have spoken to people during tests of this attack, the majority had no idea that the pin was even there or that they should never buy a gift card if the security pin has already been exposed. The other problem is that, even if the security pin has never been exposed, that doesn't mean that the gift card number can't be stolen.

I started this attack by purchasing a hand-held barcode scanner for about $75. Then I went to the grocery store, which offered dozens of different gift cards. For this particular attack, I decided I would test one specific store, Home Depot, though this attack would work on about 95% of the gift cards offered on the market today. I took every card for my test store off the rack and placed them in the top of my shopping cart. As I walked through the store seemingly shopping, I used the hand-held barcode reader to scan the barcode on each of the gift cards. When I was done, I rehung all the gift cards except for one. I purchased that card and left the store. I then went to the store and used the gift card, leaving a balance of $0 on the card. When the cashier went to take the card, I asked for it back, explaining that my son liked to play with them. The clerk gave me the empty card.

The next day, I went back to the store and scanned all the cards again. This time there were three cards missing, meaning they had been purchased. When I dumped the data at home, I was quickly able to pick out the three gift card numbers that were missing from the day before.

Now, if I were a true criminal, I would have continued my attack by using one of those three numbers. However, I am not a real bad guy, so instead, I went back to the store and purchased a second gift card.

With a razor blade, I carefully scraped the barcode and number from the used gift card I purchased a day or two earlier. I then used a printer designed to print on plastic cards to place the number from my second card onto the first card. Again, if I were a criminal, I would have printed the barcode and number for one of the cards that I knew was purchased by someone else. Now with my old card that had my newly printed barcode and number, I headed back to Home Depot. I grabbed a couple items I needed and paid using my newly printed gift card. Sure enough, the card worked like a charm, and the cashier never questioned it.

Now, some of you might be thinking to yourself, "What about that security pin?" It turns out that the security pin is only needed when you make purchases online or you use the self-checkout lines. If you check out with a live cashier, the security pin is not required, so just like that, a criminal has emptied your newly purchased gift card.

While most of the time I have security tips and suggestions on how you can protect yourself from the types of attacks I outline, in this case the real solution needs to come from the corporations making these gift cards. The real solution will come when the gift cards are properly packaged to hide the bar code as well as the security pin. Then the cashier should be required to peal off whatever has concealed the information during the time of purchase.

In the meantime, my best advice is to only purchase gift cards that have been kept behind the counter and away from places where people can easily record the numbers.

TRUTH

23

Fake charities

I am pretty certain there are few people who are more skeptical than I am when it comes to solicitations over the telephone. While I admit that I do enjoy listening to the pitch and my whole goal while on the phone is to try to knock people off their script, in the end no one can say he's ever convinced me to give him a dime.

Of course, you might jump to the conclusion that I'm cheap, but the truth of the matter is that I absolutely refuse to give out any information over the phone that would be required to make a purchase or give a donation. I just don't trust anyone. How do I know the charity is legitimate? How do I know I am not speaking to an identity thief? However, there are times when I can see how someone might just want to help those less fortunate. To those, this Truth is for you.

> How do I know I am not speaking to an identity thief?

I was probably one of the first who registered on the National Do Not Call Registry (www.donotcall.gov/). This list is designed to stop telemarketers from calling you. Of course, nothing is perfect, and I still get the occasional call, but for the most part the list really does work. However, I did notice that while the telemarketer calls stopped, calls on behalf of charities just kept coming. It turns out, when you read the fine print, the government agencies regulating the no-call list do not have jurisdiction over calls on behalf of political organizations, charities, and telephone surveyors. That means those charities can keep calling in and laying one heavy guilt trip after another. A typical call might go something like this:

> "Hello Mr. Stickley, I'm calling on behalf of the widows of fallen police officers in New York. I assume you appreciate that police officers are giving up their lives so that you can live yours...."

Seriously, how do you say no to that question? Right off the bat, you are on the hook, and now you have to figure out how to say that you can't donate $10 to help the widow buy groceries for her children. Now, just to be clear, I think police officers are far underpaid, and I have never received a traffic ticket I didn't completely deserve. That said, there is no way I am going to give a dime to this person on the phone. Just because this caller is talking about people whom we can respect and admire does not mean we have to trust the person on the line. Instead, I have found that if I am truly interested in the caller's cause, I ask for as much information as possible.

- What is the exact charity name?

- What city and state are they based out of?

- Do they have a Web site?

- What is the main contact number for the charity?

- If the caller is representing a group such as police officers, I find out if he has been endorsed by that group and where I can find more information about the endorsement.

Generally, I find that if it is truly a legitimate charity, the caller will have the answer to every one of my questions, plus offer me more information to validate who he is, while the scammer will give many excuses as to why he can't answer several of the questions. If I am truly interested in making a donation, I will let the caller know that I am onboard, and that once I have verified that the charity is legitimate, I will send a check in the mail. I do not ask for a mailing address, as I assume that when I look them up, I will be able to find that address myself.

Here are some things you should do before agreeing to give money to any charity that calls you seeking a donation.

- Verify that the charity is real. A quick visit to the IRS can help with this (http://apps.irs.gov/portal/site/pub78/). Simply type in the name of the charity, provide the city and state, and the site lets you know if they are registered.

- Make sure the charity is endorsed by the organization it is purporting to help. For instance, using the police example, if I wanted to verify the validity of the charity, I would call the police department directly and ask if it were aware of the charity in question.

- Next, perform a quick online search for the charity and verify that the Web site matches the Web site address the caller gave you.

- Send a cashier's check instead of a personal check, which contains your account number.

Generally, both real and fake charities ask you to supply a credit card or bank account number over the phone. Of course, you know by now that identity thieves can quickly and easily use both. *NEVER* give this information out, no matter how just the cause and how convincing the story.

Keep in mind that I am not saying you should stop giving. Just make sure you don't end up giving more than you planned.

Lastly, you should be aware that not all of your donation always goes to the people you think it's going to. Some more questionable charities put the majority of your donation back into "administrative fees," so the cause they represent sees little to none of your donation. That is why it is so important to speak with the group who is being represented by the charity. Many times you will find that they do not even support that charity and have set up their own charity fund and would prefer your donations go there.

24

Bogus background checks and job applications

You go online to one of the many job posting sites and find what could be the most perfect career opportunity ever. You meet all the job requirements and, more importantly, the pay looks great. You visit the company Web site and read up a little about what it does. Still excited, you submit your resume. After a few days, you receive a call expressing interest. However, before the company flies you in for an interview, it would like you to fill out an online questionnaire. You follow the provided link and answer a number of questions related to your skills. You feel that you have knocked this one out of the park.

Apparently the company agrees, since it calls you a couple days later and informs you that it is very interested in moving forward. It asks if you would be willing to take a drug test and allow the company to perform a background check. No problems there—you're drug free and fairly certain that the fender bender last year won't be held against you in the background check. The company asks you to go back to its Web site and fill out the online consent form. Once it's complete, you will be contacted within a few days to schedule for someone to come by to perform a drug test. You fill out the consent form for the background check, which requires your name, address, social security number (SSN), and driver's license number. A week later, you receive an email explaining that the position is no longer available and that your resume will be kept on record for open positions in the future.

Yes, of course, this entire process has been part of a high-tech identity theft attack. You have just given everything the identity thief would need to start his new life as you.

A number of these types of attacks have taken place all over the globe. Some are far less sophisticated attacks, in which the thief lists a simple online job posting. When the applicant replies, the thief asks for a SSN immediately. Some only use email to communicate. However, in every single case, the goal is the same—to take advantage of people while they are vulnerable and unsuspecting.

Most of the time, these attacks are aimed at nontechnical, yet high-paying jobs. Sales, marketing, and other nontechnical vocations make for prime targets. In addition, the thief pays for his bogus job posts and hosting fees using prepaid credit cards, making tracking nearly impossible. The setup of the Web site itself takes little or no time, since most are just copied from real organizations. The thief changes the company name to something bogus but leaves the majority of the site unchanged. If the site lists a toll-free number, chances are that it was purchased online by the identity thief, again with a prepaid credit card. The thief then generally has calls coming into that number forwarded to a cell phone.

As for the information that the applicant submits, it is generally forwarded via email to one of the hundreds of free email services available on the Internet. Since the thief can access these free and anonymous Web mail accounts from anywhere in the world, it, too, is largely untraceable.

Monster.com, Careerbuilder.com, and Hotjobs.com post warnings on their Web sites about these types of attacks. Yet, when I created my fake business and performed this type of attack, I found that of the 19 individuals who submitted resumes to me, 7 of them were willing to complete the online form, which included their driver's license and SSNs.

When I asked my victims why they were so willing to give the information, they said that at previous jobs, they had agreed to background checks and were required to provide the same type of information. So it only seemed normal that my scam required them to submit the same confidential information. I pointed out that at those jobs they were already hired and probably had physically been to the organization's location prior to being asked to part with such confidential personal information. But the victims of my attack said that the request to provide this kind of information just didn't seem out of the ordinary. This is exactly what identity thieves are counting on.

When it comes to protecting your identity, each new situation requires you to reevaluate what is happening with your information. Background checks have become routine with many organizations. That doesn't

The victims of my attack said that the request to provide this kind of information just didn't seem out of the ordinary. This is exactly what identity thieves are counting on.

mean that you are required to just hand over your confidential information before you ever step foot into the facility. You have just as much right to find out who is going to have access to that information and how it's going to be secured.

When applying for any job

- Never submit your SSN, driver's license number, or other personal information over the Internet.

- Understand that a professional-looking Web site and toll-free number do not guarantee it's a real company.

- Never give credit card information to employers. Period.

- If you feel you might have fallen victim to this type of attack, immediately file a fraud alert with one of the three credit reporting agencies. You can find more information about what to do if you are victimized in Part IX of this book, "The Truth About Putting a Stop to Identity Theft."

- While it is not realistic to expect the major job-posting sites to be able to guarantee that the company placing the ad is legitimate, if you come across a suspicious situation, you should notify the posting site immediately. Most sites have set up an area specifically related to security concerns.

Never give credit card information to employers.

Searching for a new job is hard enough without having to deal with someone stealing your identity during the process. As with most every identity theft attack, it all comes down to protecting your personal information.

TRUTH

25

Hotel business centers can be treacherous

Have you ever been visiting a hotel, not had your laptop with you, and needed to check email? You simply go to the hotel business center and jump on one of the computers set up for use by customers. In some cases, you have to pay a small fee to use the computers, but in most hotels, the computers are complementary to their guests. You open up the Web browser, connect to your Web mail account, type in your username and password, and just like that you are reading and responding to your emails. While you are online, you might also decide to check your bank accounts, check your brokerage site, and more. However, as you can no doubt surmise by now, like most everything else, hotel business centers are prime targets for identity thieves.

Hotel business centers are prime targets for identity thieves.

A couple of years ago, I was traveling and headed down to the hotel business center planning to log into my Web-based email via one of the public computers. When I entered the room, I sat down at a computer just after another hotel guest had finished. When I sat down, I noticed there was a Web browser already running and minimized at the bottom of the screen. I clicked on it planning to type in the URL to access my Web email. To my surprise, the window opened up to an online stock-trading Web site, with the previous user still logged in. While the obvious concern here would be that a malicious person could have started using that account and caused all sorts of trouble, I was more concerned about just how secure this computer really was that she had just used to access such confidential information.

You see, public computers are just that: public. This means that people can do just about anything they want on them. While some people browse the Web, play games, and check their email, there are those who use these computers as a point of attack to gain access to unsuspecting users' personal information.

I closed the browser that was connected to the online stock trading Web site instead of continuing with my previous plan to check my own email. Instead, I started performing an audit on the computer. I began with the obvious and downloaded an antispyware program from the Internet and ran it. Within minutes, it had found so many applications running it was simply ridiculous. While many were intrusive, none were actually designed to steal confidential information. I then ran some software to give me a complete list of all processes currently running on the computer. As I went through the list, I recognized most of the applications running with the exception of one that seemed odd. Its filename was winrunner.exe, and it was a program that was set up to start running whenever the computer booted up. I ran another program that could watch the process and noted that it was continually accessing the hard drive. After a little more research, I found a log file on the hard drive that contained a complete history of every keyboard stroke that had been entered. This included not only everything that I had typed since I had been logged in, but hundreds of entries before me, including the login information the woman had typed to access her online stocks.

Sure enough, software designed to capture potentially confidential information had been loaded on this computer by an identity thief. I immediately removed the nefarious application, typed a few more characters, and checked the log again. That time nothing more had been added to the log. I then deleted the log file to make sure it didn't end up in someone else's hands. Had I left the application running, I assume it would have emailed or transferred the log file at a predetermined time—perhaps once a day—to a waiting thief.

After this discovery, I changed my mind about using the computer to check my own mail and to this day have never used a public computer to check anything more exciting than the weather, flight times, or other information that does not require a login. Now, you might think to yourself, "What were the odds that the first computer he looked at was actually compromised?" Well, it turns out pretty darn good. Since then, I have checked more than 20 additional hotel business centers throughout the United States and have found that half of them are running malicious software designed to capture confidential information.

> I have checked more than 20 additional hotel business centers throughout the United States and have found that half of them are running malicious software.

101

The reality is that public computers are not designed to be secured access points. They are there for customer convenience only and should be used with extreme caution. As part of one of the spots I did for *The Today Show*, the hotel association was contacted by *The Today Show* at NBC. The hotel association stated that it was not responsible for securing the business center computers, and to date I have yet to see a single warning located in any hotel business center.

If you have used a public computer in the past couple months, it's time to follow some quick tips.

- Change the passwords on all the accounts you accessed through the public computer.

- If you made any online purchases via the public computer, immediately contact your credit card company and check for any suspicious activity. In addition, while it is an inconvenience, I strongly encourage you to change the credit card account number used for the transactions.

- If you used the account to access email, review all email you have received since that time and verify that you have not received anything confidential. One of the easiest types of attacks for identity thieves is to simply monitor email. Often people receive account activations and confidential information via an email. If ID thieves can access these emails, they also will gain that confidential information.

- If you accessed your business email, send out a note to your coworkers asking if they've received any emails from you recently with requests. Often thieves use a business account to send emails to other coworkers asking for confidential information on clients. If they receive a response, they record the information and then delete the email immediately, hoping that you never see it.

26

Identity thieves can hear you now...

Not all identity theft starts and ends with stealing your social security number (SSN). In fact, sometimes that is the last thing an identity thief needs. When it comes to stealing your identity, a thief really just need to know a little information about you and can then use that to gather even more. Recently, I was asked to test the security of a company that wanted to find out if a confidential database it maintained was at risk. Little did I know that this assignment would end with me exploiting Bluetooth technology in an attempt to breach this company's security.

Bluetooth technology is used in wireless communication for short distances. Most people recognize Bluetooth technology as the little devices that people hook to their ear that allow them to wirelessly answer their cell phones and carry on conversations. Most often, you notice these people because they are talking way too loudly, and generally it looks at first as though they are talking to themselves. There are a number of Bluetooth devices available that can tie into your cell phone. Models range from small portable devices that hook into your ear to devices that allow you to speak hands-free while driving.

> Not all identity theft starts and ends with stealing your SSN. Sometimes that is the last thing an identity thief needs.

For this job, I started by following an employee of the organization I was hired to test. While following this employee, I saw that he carpooled with another companion each day and that he had a Bluetooth device plugged into his cigarette lighter. Since coworkers generally do discuss business when together, especially during a commute to work, I thought chances were good that if I could manage to tap into the Bluetooth device in my mark's car, I might get the information I needed to break into his employer's database.

Joe, one of the engineers who I work with, wrote some code that could communicate with Bluetooth devices. However, as we started to test the code, we found that some devices require the user to manually put them into pairing mode, which then allows other devices to be able to "see" them and make a connection. Some devices also require a PIN to be submitted, which provides an additional level of security. This was obviously not what I was looking for. But just when I started to think that I might not be able to listen in through the device, Joe made a huge discovery.

It turned out that many of the devices that are made for placement in a car actually remain in pairing mode at all times. Also, these devices have a default PIN that can't be changed. In other words, there was a chance that I might be able to connect to that Bluetooth device after all.

After some research, I learned that most auto manufacturers had secured their devices by 2007, but that more than half of the devices available today are actually vulnerable to this type of attack.

More than half of the devices available today are actually vulnerable to this type of attack.

So I studied pictures of all the devices and later peeked inside my target's car and discovered that the device he used was vulnerable to this kind of attack. The next day, I sat in a nearby parking lot with my Bluetooth-equipped laptop and a modified antenna. As my victim started his car, the Bluetooth device turned on, and my computer connected to the victim's Bluetooth device.

Sure enough, I was able to listen to everything being said in the car (not just what was said on the phone). I followed them home, attempting to stay as close as possible. The range was no more than one or two car lengths, and I lost the connection if another car was between me and the car I was tailing. I followed them for the next several days, recording all their conversations. It was clear they were completely unaware that I was listening in.

Unfortunately, while I recorded some interesting conversations, the confidential information I was required to gather never came up, and I turned my attention to other means of attack.

So why have I shared all this with you if it turned out to be a complete bust? While I was unsuccessful in obtaining the information I needed to complete the job I was hired to perform, I found that I actually could have easily gone after the individuals in the car. On one occasion, the passenger was talking on the phone purchasing flowers. During the call, he gave his name, address, and credit card information. While this was dumb luck that I happened to be recording this information at that time, it still proved that if a thief is persistent, he can harvest confidential information by monitoring your Bluetooth phone.

Because there is no fix for the devices that are vulnerable to this type of attack, I can only give advice on how to avoid vulnerable Bluetooth devices.

- When purchasing a hands-free Bluetooth device, make sure that the device requires you to press a button before it goes into pairing mode. Generally, the higher-priced models require that you press a button to enter pairing mode, but this wasn't the case with every device I studied. Make sure the device you buy requires that you manually engage pairing mode to use it with your cell phone.

- If you already have a device that remains in constant pairing mode, my only suggestion is to leave it turned off until you need to make a call. Since most devices allow only one connection at a time, this gives you additional security. When the call is complete, make sure to turn the device off.

- Some devices allow you to change their configuration to disable automatic pairing. Check your user's manual, and if possible, disable the automatic pairing feature.

- In the early 2000s, some automobiles came with Bluetooth built in and are also vulnerable to this type of attack. If your automobile has automatic pairing enabled, contact your dealer to see if it can supply a fix.

- Not sure if your device supports auto pairing? Turn the device on and then, using a friend's cell phone, attempt to connect via Bluetooth to the device. If your friend can connect without your needing to press any buttons on the device, your device is at risk.

TRUTH

27

ATM scams

Throughout this book, I have discussed a variety of ways in which identity thieves have devised to separate you from your hard-earned cash. Thieves use everything from brute force to subterfuge to confidence schemes to technological wizardry to steal your money and perhaps even your identity. So by now it should come as no shock that identity thieves will even go so far as to set up a fake ATM to empty your bank account.

Identity thieves have used numerous techniques to attempt to gain people's PINs. In some cases, they've placed a small camera hidden somewhere on the ATM. In one example, the thief made a fake flyer holder containing a tiny camera that was attached to the ATM. A small hole had been drilled into the holder so that the camera could see and record users entering their PINs. In other cases, thieves have taken a lower-tech approach and just sat near the ATM and used a high-powered lens to watch as people entered their PIN.

While fake ATMs got their start back in the early 1990s, most people have never given them a second thought. In fact, because ATMs now come in every size, shape, and color, most people would be hard pressed to know the difference between a real ATM and a fake one. With this in mind, I decided to see just how easy it would be to run this attack myself.

First, I decided I would try to purchase an ATM machine on eBay. While I did find ATM machines I could purchase, they were more expensive than I expected. And I thought even if I did purchase an ATM, I would have to reprogram it. So I decided to build my fake ATM.

After more searching, I discovered a college that was selling four large metal kiosks. The kiosks were seven feet tall and had plenty of room for a small monitor and keyboard. After winning the auction, I had the kiosks shipped to my corporate office, where several of our engineers got to work on them. We ordered large "No Fees!" stickers to cover the sides and front. I also ordered touch-screen monitors and magnetic strip readers. One of my engineers changed out the keyboard shelves and placed a nice sticker atop it indicating the types of cards that were accepted.

Once completed, my ATMs looked just like the real thing—at least at first glance. Had people paid close attention, they would have noticed there was nowhere for the money to come out, and there was no way to get a receipt. I assumed since this machine was never going to give money or receipts, no one would ever be looking.

Next, we wrote a basic program that would provide screen prompts for the user to insert a card, enter a PIN, and enter a transaction. Since the whole idea here was to prove that this could be done and not to actually steal anything, the program recorded only the last four digits of the account number and simply counted the digits in the PIN.

I now had several fully operational ATM identity theft devices. We loaded two of the machines into a rental truck and took them on the road. We ended up placing them in Austin, Texas, on 6th Street. This busy street is known for its many bars and nightclubs. My goal was to see if anyone would become suspicious and, of course, if anyone would actually use them.

To say that we had success would be an understatement. In just under five hours, we were able to capture 27 card numbers and could've captured the PINs if we'd wanted them. This means that had I been a real identity thief, I would have been able to take that information, make my own fake ATM cards, and go out on a shopping spree.

> To say that we had success would be an understatement. In just under five hours, we were able to capture 27 partial card numbers.

Of course, because the machine couldn't dispense money, as soon as it was apparent that the user had been duped, I told them about the "scam." Interestingly, even after the machine had failed to process the transaction, the victims never thought there was anything malicious going on. When I pointed out obvious flaws, such as the missing money feeder, the victims would laugh and say they couldn't believe they had missed that important detail. The comment I heard repeatedly was, "How can we tell a real ATM from a fake when they all look so different?" It's a valid question without a simple answer.

Instead, I can merely offer a number of tips that, when combined, can help protect you from falling victim to this type of attack.

- Beware if the ATM doesn't charge fees. Private ATMs not associated directly with banks (often seen in service stations and bars) make their money through fees. While it's possible that there could be a privately owned no-fee ATM out there somewhere, it's definitely something to raise an eyebrow.

- Look around. Is the ATM free standing? While ATMs can be anywhere, you want to avoid the ATM that is freestanding outside. Avoid ATMs that are not bolted to the side of a building or secured inside a facility. If you can walk up and start pushing the ATM down the street, this is generally a bad sign.

- Take action if the ATM failed to process your transaction. Most ATMs do not allow you to attempt to sign in when they are out of service. Instead, nonfunctioning ATMs post a message onscreen indicating that they are down or offline. If the ATM shows an error message after you have submitted your card and your PIN, contact your bank immediately to report what happened.

- Follow the layered approach. For example, if the machine offers no fees but it is attached to a building and everything processes properly, you are probably fine. It's when you start seeing several of these tips combined that you should be seriously concerned.

- If you use an ATM that doesn't dispense cash, you are at far greater risk that it was a fake and should notify your bank of the potential risk to your account.

- Pay close attention to the slot you slide in your card. If it looks strange or bulky, try to push on it with your hand. If something has been stuck over the real reader, it will wiggle or even come off. If you spot one of these, most likely, it's a device that an identity thief placed on the ATM to read your card as you place it into the ATM slot.

- Always be aware of your physical surroundings. Using an ATM late at night in an empty parking lot is asking for trouble. Also, it's a good idea to shield the keypad with your hand as you enter your PIN to prevent a hidden camera from capturing your information.

28

Wireless access scams

You have just checked into a hotel while on a business trip. After getting settled, you decide to use the hotel's wireless access to check your email and maybe get a little work done. You open your Web browser, and instead of connecting to your familiar home page, it instead connects to a Web page supplied by the hotel. The hotel offers Internet access for $12.99 per day. Since you plan to only be online for an hour or two, this seems pretty ridiculous. You click on your wireless icon again to see if you can locate another wireless network you can use. You scroll down the list and see an unsecured access point named "WiFly." You select it, and within a few seconds you are connected.

You open a new Web browser and once again you are redirected to a different Web page. This time the page displays a message from the company WiFly, which also charges for access, though the cost is only $1.99 per day. You fill out the online form with your name, credit card type, credit card number, expiration date, and the 3-digit security code on the back of the card. Once approved, you are redirected to a WiFly home page confirming your connection.

You now attempt to connect to your Web mail site. As the page starts to load, a security warning pops up explaining that there is a problem with the site's security certificate and asks if you would like to proceed. Thinking maybe you mistyped the address, you select No, close your browser, reopen the browser, and try to reconnect to your Web mail page. Once again, the same message pops up. This time, you select Yes to continue. The correct page comes up, and everything looks normal. In addition, the lock icon in your task tray is locked, indicating that the page is encrypted. You also note that the site address begins with https:, indicating that you are on a secured site. Once you have verified that your connection is secure, you log in into your mail account with your username and password. Sure enough, everything works great, and you read all your new emails. When you are done, you log out. You continue to browse for another hour or two, and every once in a while that same security certificate message pops up, but by now you have realized there is just something wrong with your connection, so you just ignore those, selecting Yes each time.

Unfortunately, when your credit card statement arrives, you find that thousands of dollars in fraudulent charges have been racked up on your card.

It turns out that the company, WiFly, didn't really exist. The connection that was made via wireless really went to a wireless device that had been set up in another room located somewhere in the hotel. When you entered your credit card information, you actually submitted it to an identity thief who was sitting nearby recording it. The identity thief then just passed the connection to the Internet back through his own computer in what is known as a man-in-the-middle design. This means that everything you, the victim, did was actually passing through the identity thief's computer and then through to the Internet.

Remember that security warning that kept popping up? That was because all your Web traffic was actually being redirected first to the identity thief's computer, decrypted, logged, and then reencrypted and passed on to its final destination. That warning was real, and the only thing that could protect you from falling victim. Once you chose to continue, you chose to ignore the warning and put your information at risk.

I performed tests with this type of attack in airports, hotels, coffee shops, and book stores. In most cases, I offered the service for a small fee. I was able to easily gather credit card and other personal information. During some of these tests, I would ask for social security numbers (SSN) as well. I was amazed at the success I had. While gathering the credit cards proved that identity thieves could be successful with this type of attack, obtaining the SSNs proved this attack could be even more dangerous.

In addition, I had the ability to gather login credentials for email and online banking accounts, chat programs, online business applications, and various other online services. Had I been a real identity thief, this information would have been used for numerous attacks.

Had I been a real identity thief, this information would have been used for numerous attacks.

Because this type of attack can happen anywhere that you connect via a wireless connection, it is extremely important that you follow a few simple guidelines.

- If you have a choice between using wireless and plugging into an actual wire, choose the wire. You should be able to assume the wire is plugged into the hotel's network, so you know for certain you are using its connection. While this is far more secure, this connection does not guarantee 100% privacy. Note: Other risks come into play if you choose to use the hotel business center. See Truth 25.

- Choose to connect to the service offered by the establishment you are visiting. If you are at a hotel, use the service it advertises in the room. Attempting to save a buck by using a different service provider may end up costing you more in the long run.

- If you are required to use a credit card to purchase service, try to use a card that has a low credit limit and, more importantly, never user your bank debit card. Because a bank debit card draws directly from your bank account, if this number is stolen, your cash can be drained quickly and could take a while before you are able to have it reimbursed. With a credit card, however, you are not required to pay any bogus charges while they are being investigated.

- If you receive a security warning that indicates the security certificate has an issue of any kind, do not continue. I cannot stress this enough. A legitimate Web site should never have an invalid security certificate. When in doubt, contact the company via phone and explain what is happening. If you select to continue, you will not receive any additional warnings while at that Web site, and you may be putting your confidential information at risk.

- A free wireless access point can be just as dangerous as a pay service. While you may not have given credit card information, you may still be at risk of your connection being monitored and your personal information being stolen.

29

Credit card skimming

Have you ever wondered why there seems to be no rhyme or reason as to when you are asked to show ID when using a credit card?

At many of the grocery stores and major retail outlets, you actually swipe your own card, never even handing it the cashier. In some cases, after you swipe the card and approve the amount, a message displays on the screen telling you to show the card to the cashier; however, the cashier rarely looks. Other times, diligent cashiers do ask to see your ID. What's more amusing is that if you go through the regular line, cashiers ask for ID when you use the credit card; however, if you use self-checkout, there is no one available to check your ID, so there's no validation. I don't think I am giving a criminal any hot tip when I point this out. I have also noticed that some merchants no longer even require a signature for credit card purchases totaling less than $20.

With all the identity theft and credit card fraud that is taking place around the globe, you have to assume that the credit card companies must be getting angry at the merchants who are failing to perform proper ID validation. However, you would be wrong.

In fact, the actual guidelines from the major credit card companies seem to be ambiguous at best. In the worst case, they actually insist that merchants not ask for ID when accepting a credit card. Apparently, credit cards are to be treated as cash. While treating credit like cash sounds nice, we live in a world in which identity theft is out of control. While I might carry $100 cash with me occasionally, I am quite certain that most people are not carrying $10,000 in their purses and wallets. So to treat credit the same as cash is to assume that people would absorb the same risk with both.

> With all the identity theft and credit card fraud that is taking place around the globe, you have to assume that the credit card companies must be getting angry... you would be wrong.

Obviously, if someone steals your credit card, he or she is going to spend far more than the $100 cash in your pocket. The point is that the system is broken, insecure, and ultimately leaves you to fend for your own credit security. And it's this general lack of control that has made credit card skimming a lucrative practice for identity thieves.

The term skimming refers to taking a legitimate credit card and making a copy of the card without the owner's knowledge. Identity thieves often get involved with employees at restaurants and bars working out a deal in which the employee skims the cards and the identity thief pays for the stolen numbers. So how easy is it?

I have tested this type of attack in several locations and found it was frighteningly easy. I started by picking up an inexpensive, easy-to-use magnetic strip read/write device from the Internet.

In my first test, a friend let me pose as a bartender in his bar. When a patron paid with a credit card, I would swipe the card through the bar's card machine and then swipe it through my own card reader that I had set up to capture information right off the cards.

In another test, I concealed a small camera inside my hand, which was wrapped with a bandage. When I went to several bars, I was able to scan cards lying on the bar by simply passing my hand over the card. The camera would record the name, number, and expiration date.

Next, I decided to see what happened if I copied my own credit card information onto other cards. I actually used hotel room key cards and copied my credit card information onto them using my magnetic strip reader/writer.

After making my new cards, I went to a store that allows you to swipe your own credit card. The transaction with my modified hotel key card was approved and, as expected, the cashier didn't ask to see the card. Had I been a real thief, all the card numbers I had gathered at the bars could have been used for this attack.

Next, I went to a location that I knew would ask for ID. I swiped the card and then waited. Sure enough, the cashier asked to see the card and my ID. I handed her the room key and my ID, and her expression was priceless. She asked me for the credit card, and I told her that was the credit card. She called over a manager. The manager explained that he needed the original credit card, and I explained that for my security and privacy, I only carried room keys that contained my card information.

In the end, the store did let me make the purchase after carefully looking at my ID again. I didn't have the same good luck when I tried this everywhere. One location took one look at the card and canceled my order. I was told to use a real credit card, and when I started to get upset, the store offered to call the police. I chose to leave.

Here is what I suggest to protect yourself.

- When paying with a credit card, never leave the card laying out for the public to see. While many restaurants provide a holder to place your card in when they leave the bill, often times bars simply leave the receipt lying in front of you. In that case, place the credit card under the receipt partially sticking out.

- It's rare that you can see where your card is taken after your server picks it up. But in the event that he does stay in your sight, pay attention. If you see him swipe the card more than one time, or if you see him writing anything down while he is looking at your card, be concerned. I would even go so far as to ask him what he was writing or why he scanned it twice. If it was malicious, generally the fact that you called the server out on it will be enough to deter him from using your card.

- Most credit card companies allow you to set up an email limit notification. You can set a number, and when your credit card balance goes over that number, you will receive an email letting you know. I suggest keeping this number low enough to be a safety net while not so low as to be hit with normal usage. If you are notified that you're over the limit, it could be your first indication that your card has been stolen.

- Never use your banking ATM debit card for purchases at restaurants, bars, and other locations where the card is taken out of your sight. Unlike a credit card, the debit card pulls funds directly from your banking account. And, unlike a credit card account in which you can decline to pay for items that are under investigation as fraud, when you use a debit card, the cash is removed immediately.

TRUTH

30

PayPal scams

Sometimes identity thieves realize that they need help to pull off the perfect score. And sometimes the identity the thief is pilfering is not that of a person, but that of an entire business. This Truth is based on actual events that occurred when a coworker of mine decided to sell his laptop on Craigslist.com.

Myles is a security engineer I work with at TraceSecurity. He recently had been given a new laptop by the company, so he no longer needed his personal laptop he had bought just a few months earlier. Like millions of other people, he decided to sell it on Craigslist.

Myles posted a simple ad stating the details of the laptop and an approximate asking price. After a few days, he received an email from someone who said she was very interested in purchasing it. Not only that, she told him she would be willing to pay extra if he would ship it to her in another state even though he had offered it for local pickup only. Being the entrepreneur that he is, Myles accepted the increased offer.

> Sometimes the identity the thief is pilfering is not that of a person, but that of an entire business.

A couple days later, Myles received the confirmation email from PayPal indicating the funds had been received for the laptop. Also, the buyer emailed the shipping address to him. Since the buyer had paid almost $100 more than the original packing price, Myles put extra effort into bubble wrapping the device to make sure it traveled well. All that was left to do was drop the box in the mail, and the transaction was complete.

However, being one of the many paranoid people who have passed through the halls of our company, Myles couldn't help but think that something just didn't seem right. Sure, the buyer had seemed pretty cool in the emails they had exchanged, and more importantly had already paid through PayPal, so what was the problem?

Well, fortunately for Myles, the paranoia was justified. On a whim, he logged into PayPal and reviewed all recent payments to his account. As he looked through the list, the payment for his laptop seemed to be missing. This was rather odd, as once he had received a payment via PayPal, he wouldn't expect it to then disappear. Also, had the funds been removed, there should still have been a log of the events. He then thought that maybe he had been mistaken about the verification email he had received from PayPal confirming the payment for the laptop. He went back and looked again. Sure enough, the email was there, and indeed PayPal had confirmed the funds.

At this point, it all started to become clear. The buyer had never actually paid anything. Instead, the buyer simply impersonated PayPal by sending the confirmation letter on PayPal's behalf. Had Myles just accepted the phony email without additional review, he would have been out one laptop.

But the story doesn't end there. Once this was brought to my attention, I thought it would be fun to track down the buyer and let the police take care of business. After making some calls and getting law enforcement involved, we were able to trace the delivery address to a small town in the Midwest. When we spoke to the town sheriff, he was perplexed. It turned out that not only did he know the address the laptop was to be delivered to, he lived on the same street and knew the family who lived there. During the call, he informed us that the home was occupied by a husband, his wife, and their 16-year-old son. Immediately, we focused on the son, though the sheriff did make a point several times during the call to say how surprised he was about the situation, as the boy had never been in trouble before and seemed like a good kid. I have met identity thieves who were extremely likable and charming, so this was not a surprise to me.

What did surprise me is the next call that came from the sheriff. Instead of the son being out to make a quick buck, it turned out that it was his mother. The sheriff had stopped by the home of the boy just to let the parents know what was going on. While he was explaining the situation, the mom grew silent, and by the time he was done, the mom was in tears.

Mom had recently found a job on the Internet where she could earn money while working from home. All she had to do was ship equipment that was sent to her home to a mailing address overseas. For her efforts, she would be paid cash or could keep items for herself. So when the thief impersonated PayPal and had Myles send his laptop to this woman's home, she in turn would've shipped it to another country. Had all this happened, Myles would have been after the woman in the Midwest and not the real thief living overseas. Ultimately, the mom learned a valuable lesson, and the real thief got away without so much as a warning. Fortunately, protecting yourself from this type of attack requires only basic due diligence.

- Never trust an email verifying that funds have been deposited into your account. Before you ship the item, simply log into your online account and verify that the funds have truly been deposited.

- While there are many legitimate business opportunities that you can find online, always research the employer. Make sure the employer's address is in the same country in which you reside and that it is not a P.O. box. Make sure that the phone number is local and, if possible, get a tax ID number, which should help you verify that the organization is real, not a front for a thief.

> Before you ever ship the item, simply log into your online account and verify that the funds have truly been deposited.

Remember that identity theft can take many different forms. It is just as easy to impersonate a business as it is to impersonate a person. Luckily, the solution is almost always the same. Simply take the time to verify the information being presented.

31

Email scams

You open your email and find that you are the recipient of an email purporting to be from a Nigerian prince who also happens to be a senior-level accountant with a Nigerian oil company. The general gist of the letter is that you are asked to allow this accountant to temporarily stash surplus money in your U.S. bank account. Of course, the letter indicates that you will be paid handsomely for your assistance. All you need to do is supply your bank account number and then sit back as you rake in the big bucks.

Now, if you are like me, you immediately begin to laugh. But for some, it's no joking matter. Many people have fallen for this scam, and there does not seem to be an end in sight. The original Nigerian scam actually started back in the 1980s as a postal mail scam, migrated to fax machines, and now thrives in the cyberworld. Why? Because the letters continue to change, and the attacks continue to become more sophisticated.

When I receive one of these emails, I immediately respond using one of my many alias email addresses. Using my aliases, I can be young, old, man, or woman. In some cases, I send a few separate emails to the same thief using different aliases. My goal is to see just how far these thieves are willing to go to steal from me. Of course, I assume the endgame is to get my cash, but I have found that many times thieves running this scam are just as interested in getting my account numbers, social security numbers (SSN), and in some cases even my driver's license number. What I have also found is that there is no limit to the amount of time and effort they are willing to put into the attack.

> There is no limit to the amount of time and effort they are willing to put into the attack.

On one occasion, I was corresponding with the "Nigerian official" and expressed interest in helping him with his cause. He was polite, and as we exchanged emails, he informed me that he was on a tight time schedule. He would need to get the funds transferred into my account quickly. Of course, I was eager to help expedite matters. He asked for my bank account information so that he would be able to transfer the funds directly to me. I told him I was a little concerned about giving him this information since I didn't know him personally and couldn't be sure that the money he promised me actually existed. Surprisingly, he said he understood and that he would contact someone at the bank to set me up with online access to the account so that I could verify it myself.

He also told me he was a little concerned about transferring such a large amount of money to me, but he had no choice and would just have to trust me. Two days later, I received another email containing the link to an online bank, a username, and a password. At this point, I honestly was starting to wonder what was going on. I followed the link, and sure enough it was a bank located in Nigeria. I was able to log into the account and see that there was more than $20 million sitting in the account. Now, I was really starting to see how someone could get sucked into this type of attack.

After I started to poke around a little, I soon discovered that the bank site was bogus, of course, and that it had only been live for a couple of days. In fact, when I dug a little deeper, I saw that the site contained little more than a home page, a login screen, and a phony account balance page. There were no other options other than to display a balance, and if I entered the incorrect password, the account still logged in. That said, I still was impressed that the schemer had gone to such trouble to pull this off.

Ultimately, I gave him bogus account information, and shortly after I never heard from him again. Had I given him a real bank account number, you can rest assured that any funds in that account would have been picked clean in a day.

In other communications with the "Nigerian officials," I have been asked for my SSN or driver's license number to verify my identity and the location to which they would be sending this large amount of money. Of course, all these attempts were aimed at using my personal information to commit identity theft.

Some people who have been sucked into this scam actually have received cashier's checks for large sums of money. The "Nigerian official" would send the check to the victims explaining that, though he could send a cashier's check, he could not directly put the money into another account. He explained that the other account needed to have money wired into it for the larger sum to be released. When the victims received the cashier's check and deposited it in the bank without incident, they were immediately convinced everything was legitimate and then wire transferred a portion of that money back to the designated account. However, what these victims didn't realize is that a cashier's check is not the same as cash, and there are no guarantees it won't bounce. It could take your bank several weeks to verify the funds, during which time the funds will show as being in your account.

The most obvious advice I can give you is that no one will ever randomly contact you and offer to give you hundreds of thousands of dollars—ever. However, here are a few other tips.

- A cashier's check is not cash and is not guaranteed. If you deposit the check, do not use any of that money until your bank has told you the check has cleared. (This could take several weeks.)

- Never give your banking account information to someone via email or over the phone. If this person is offering to deposit funds into your account, have him send you a check or use Western Union to wire the money to you.

- The email will not always come from Nigeria. It may come from a lottery official, special charity group, government entity, or some poor soul claiming to be looking for help. No matter what the case, the best rule of thumb is to simply delete the email. No matter how real it looks, no matter how nice the person is, I promise you, it's only going to cost you in the end.

> No matter how real it looks, no matter how nice the person is, I promise you, it's only going to cost you in the end.

There is one last note that I think should be made clear. The Nigerian scam has led to actual physical harm, as these scammers often attempt to convince the victims to actually travel to Nigeria. Again, all I can say is "delete."

TRUTH

32

Online shopping scams

The proliferation of online shopping has created a fertile hunting ground for identity thieves. All it takes is a little Web-site savvy, the promise of bargain prices, and a few dollars in site hosting fees, and the thief is in business. As you've no doubt learned already, making a fake Web site can take as little as 20 minutes for the skilled identity thief. Often, the thief will simply copy a real Web site and then change the information needed to make it his own. The thief will then entice you to "order" from him by offering prices far lower than other stores and perhaps even offering hard-to-find items during the holidays (gaming console systems, the hot children's toy of the season, and so on).

When I conducted my own tests with this attack, I made a site that targeted people looking for the Nintendo Wii game system, which helped drive buyers to my site. Using Google ads, I advertised a low price, which I knew would bring in the buyers. Sure, I had to pay to get my ad to be circulated, but were I a true identity thief, the small amount invested would be well worth it for the payout in the end. Within minutes of my ad hitting the Internet, I started getting traffic.

I had seen firsthand just how easy it was for an identity thief to capture credit card information.

I have to admit that my site was nothing fancy, and I had assumed that people might grow suspicious because of the poor quality. But to my surprise, it seemed that most buyers didn't notice. Because I was offering a great price on a then hard-to-find item, the credit card numbers started to roll in. Obviously, I am not an identity thief, and I didn't want to ruin Christmas for anyone, so for my tests, I only recorded the last 4 digits of the credit card number as well as the contact name and phone number. Also, when buyers clicked the Submit button, a pop-up message appeared telling them that currently we were out of stock, so the order could not be processed and the credit card would not be charged.

After a couple days, I had more than 30 attempted purchases and 200 visits. I imagine if I had put more effort into the Web site, my purchase rate would have been even higher. But for testing purposes, I had more than enough information. I had seen firsthand just how easy it was for an identity thief to capture credit card information.

I called a few of my victims to discuss the theft. Every victim told me the price was too good to pass up. I asked if they had noticed that the Web site was a little low budget, and one of them told me he assumed that we probably didn't care about our site design since we knew our prices were so good.

When shopping online, you really have no idea who is on the other side of the transaction. Obviously, you can feel comfortable with the big online retailers, such as Amazon and Netflix, or the brick-and-mortar stores, such as Sears or Wal-Mart. The same can't be said for some of the no-name Web sites that are selling sweaters to raise money for the homeless. How do you know it's safe to give your credit card, and is it truly worth the risk? Let me answer the second part of that question first. The simple answer is yes, if you have found a great deal or an item that you just have to have, it is worth the risk. Now, that said, I am not a big fan of risk and would rather just attempt to prove the site is safe.

■ Make sure the site is using a security certificate. When you visit any site that requires confidential information, you will notice that the URL changes from http:// to https://. In addition, if you are using Internet Explorer 6 or Mozilla Firefox, you will see a picture of a closed lock in the bottom-right side of your browser. This lock is not in the Web page but in the frame of the browser. (In some cases, malicious sites try to trick visitors by just putting a picture of a lock in the Web page.) In Internet Explorer 7, the lock is located on the top in the location bar. Being a secured site does not guarantee complete safety, but it does mean the site has filed for a security certificate, paid a fee, and given some verified contact information.

> When shopping online, you really have no idea who is on the other side of the transaction.

- Look up how long the Web site domain has existed. The newer the site, the more you are at risk. To look up the domain, visit www.networksolutions.com and select the WHOIS Search option. Type in the domain name such as amazon.com, and WHOIS pulls up all the information for that domain. If the creation date is less than a year old, I generally shy away. On the flip side, just because it may be two or three years old doesn't guarantee you can trust it.

- Watch for poor Web site design, including broken links and missing images. Much like I was not willing to put the time into making a great-looking Web site, many real thieves will feel the same.

- Check for a contact phone number, and attempt to call it. If you can't reach a real person, you may wonder how you will be taken care of should there be a problem with your merchandise.

- Legitimate sites often have received certificates that are posted on their home page. Click on the link, and make sure it takes you back to the site that certified it. That site should list information about the company, including its domain. If they do not match, you should not trust the site. (In some complex scams, however, fake certificates and Web sites are also made to add to the illusion.)

- Check for business partners listed on the site and contact them to get feedback about the company.

Of course, a site could meet every criterion I listed and still be malicious. This is where I have one last piece of advice for the online shopper: Never use your banking debit card to make purchases online. While a credit card is easy to challenge bogus charges, with a debit card the money is coming directly out of your bank account. This means that your account could be bone dry before you ever realize that there is a problem. Instead, use a dedicated credit card that has a lower limit, and make sure to check the billing statement carefully each month.

Never use your banking debit card to make purchases online.

TRUTH

33

Fake e-card greetings

When I was first dating my wife, I remember receiving an e-card from her. I clicked the link, and it brought up a Web page that played a short video of a dancing dog expressing its love for me. While it was a little corny, it was funny, and I was amused. For those who have never received an e-card, my assumption is you are probably already married. This assumption is based on my own life, in which once I said, "I do," the e-cards stopped.

You are sitting at your computer and a new email comes in. The subject line reads, "You have a Hallmark e-card greeting!" It's from ecards@hallmark-ecard.com, and the letter invites you to click on the link provided in the note to see your card.

You click on the link, and the Hallmark Web site comes up with the familiar logo, as well as several menu options for the online store and more. In the middle of the page, you notice an error message in bold that reads, "To use this product, you need to install free software." The message provides simple instructions.

After following the instructions and clicking Refresh, your e-card begins to play. The card ends with a note telling you that you have a secret admirer who thinks you're neat. Unfortunately, the only person who thinks you're neat right now is your identity thief.

When I was writing this book, I sometimes thought that you might be reading each Truth in the same way that I watch a magician at the mall. My goal is to spot the exact moment the trick takes place. He points at something with his left hand while his right hand quickly slips in and out of his pocket. Everyone is supposed to be watching the left hand, but for those who don't follow the misdirection, they think, "A-ha! It just happened with that right hand."

I think something similar happens in these bogus Web sites. You read the page and see that you are directed to install software. You should be thinking, "A-ha! There it is. There is the hand in the pocket." But much like the magician at the mall, the misdirection is set the minute you lose focus on

The misdirection is set the minute you lose focus on the potential risk and instead focus on the excitement of a secret admirer.

the potential risk and instead focus on the excitement of a secret admirer.

While it's true that you did indeed receive an e-card and eventually it really is coming from Hallmark, the attack happened in between.

I have re-created this attack by visiting Hallmark's site, creating an e-card from a secret admirer, and sending it to myself. I then created my own Web site, which is a carbon copy of Hallmark's Web site. The only difference is that the real Hallmark store is located at hallmark. com, while I used the link hallmark-ecard.com. Then I sent emails to my victims, who followed the link to my Web site.

My site looks to see if the "special software" is already loaded. If not, the user is instructed to load it. If the software is installed, the user has fallen victim to my attack before, so my Web site simply redirects him to the real Hallmark Web site and points him to the video that I had originally sent from the secret admirer.

When the user chooses to load that software that was supposed to be the Hallmark Video Viewer, he is really loading malicious software that is designed to compromise the computer. Through the years, I have used numerous payloads depending on who was being targeted. If I am attacking a home user, my goal is to load software that captures his keyboard strokes. This allows me to record usernames and passwords tied to online applications, including online banking. The software may also steal cookies and other files from the victim's computer.

When attacking an organization, my goal is often to gain access to the corporate network. Since most organizations have software in place to stop a hacker from getting into the network via the Internet, it makes far more sense to target employees and have them open the access from the inside. When the employee loads the Video Viewer software on his computer, it "calls home" using a technique known as a reverse Telnet.

While the technical details are not relevant, the ultimate outcome is the user's computer starting what appears to be a Web connection from his computer with a computer on the Internet. When the connection is made, the computer then hands control of that connection to the receiving computer on the Internet, often with full administrator access. This means that the hacker is now sitting at the malicious computer on the Internet and can start typing commands. Whatever is typed is run on the user's computer at the organization. This allows a hacker to not only steal data from that computer, but also use that computer as a launching point to attack other computers on that internal corporate network.

Through the years, I have used this particular attack thousands of times against both home users and employees at corporations with over a 95 percent success rate.

While these attacks can be devastating, they are fairly easy to prevent.

■ Never install software unless you are absolutely certain you know what it does and who created it. This will be your hardest rule to follow since there are times you are required to load software when visiting Web sites.

■ When installing software, watch for publisher security alerts. When you elect to install a program in Windows, a security warning appears telling you who published and certified the product. If the warning reads "Unknown Publisher," it's the only warning that Microsoft can give you that you may not want to trust this product. If you choose to continue to install, you are taking complete responsibility.

■ Even having a validated publisher doesn't guarantee the software is safe. In fact, a number of malicious codes have received valid certificates. If you are suspicious, I would suggest following that gut instinct and choosing not to load it.

■ By default, an email from Hallmark contains the real sender's email address. If the email comes from an unknown source, don't open it.

■ This attack is not exclusive to Hallmark and can be done with any site that contains any kind of multimedia. Much like phishing, when you receive any link in an email, you need to immediately be suspicious.

TRUTH

34

Rogue wireless access points

You're at work, feeling a bit burned out or bored, and want to chat with a friend online. Unfortunately, your company has blocked all chat sites. Of course, you start wondering if there is another chat program available that your company hasn't blocked yet. After searching for awhile, you find that your company has really done its homework and blocked every chat program you can find. That's when it hits you. Your laptop has wireless capabilities built right into it.

You bring up a list of potential wireless access points that are in range of your office. Some of them appear to be secured, but you come across one labeled "Linksys" that doesn't require a password. You give it a shot, and the connection attempt fails. Then you remember that your office has set up a default Internet gateway that you use while in the office. So it stands to reason that you won't be able to connect to this new wireless network unless you remove the default gateway that your IT department set up. After you do that, you connect to the wireless network without a hitch, and suddenly, the Internet is yours. You can chat, visit any site you like, and behave as though you were surfing from your computer at home.

If you are an employee who may have become a little creative in gaining access to the Internet on your company's network, I encourage you to stop.

If you're an IT manager, your stomach has probably just knotted up because you can already guess where this is going to end up. For those of you who aren't techie, it's important to understand that the IT manager who had placed all those restrictions on the network put them there as a major part of your company's network security. In fact, for each minute that you continue to be connected to that rogue wireless access point, not only are you putting your own computer and possibly your identity in jeopardy, but you are also putting the entire corporate network at risk.

A law firm I once worked with asked me to test its internal security. Like the fictitious company I described at the beginning of this Truth, this law firm's IT department had locked down its access to allow only email communication and limited Web access. While I was onsite, I noticed some strange traffic coming from one of the computers on the network. I asked to be taken to that computer, so I could find out what was going on. It turned out to be the laptop of one of the attorneys, who was defensive when I asked him if I could look at his computer. I explained that his computer seemed to be running malicious software on the network and I was concerned that it might be compromised. Finally, the attorney relented and let me take a look. It turned out that he had been connected to a third-party wireless access point and had been using it for the past several months. Because he had been connected to this rogue wireless access point while also connected to the company's internal network, his computer had been compromised and was being used without his knowledge to infiltrate the rest of the organization's network.

Most companies use a firewall to protect their computers from the outside world. Firewalls prevent computers on the inside of the firewall from being accessed by anyone outside the company network. Because this layer of security exists, even if your computer on the network has a potential security flaw, hackers can never touch it. System administrators rely heavily on the firewall as a primary line of defense for keeping their networks safe. However, if you set your computer to connect to the Internet using a different path, such as a random wireless access point, you have just lost that primary line of defense.

Because that compromised laptop was also still connected to the law firm's internal network, the user had basically become a conduit allowing the hacker to access his computer through the wireless side and subsequently attack other computers on the wired corporate side. Fortunately for the law firm, the hacker never gained access to the primary database. However, the hacker was able to gain access to the employee's online bank account, his Netflix account, several pending case files, as well as all his email correspondence.

Employees often do not understand the risks of disabling the security measures that their companies have taken. More importantly, IT personnel rarely explain the limitations that they pose on users. This creates tension as users start to make their own assumptions and eventually look to subvert those security measures.

137

So when limiting access on your network, follow these simple tips.

- **Don't block too much.** There is a balance between protecting a network and becoming a dictator. If employees can't access information needed to at least do their jobs, they will become creative, which could ultimately put your network at greater risk.

- **Explain the risks to your employees.** No one wants to be hacked. Ensure that employees understand that the security controls in place serve an important purpose. Make certain they understand the layers of security on your network and the risks if those layers are bypassed.

- **Make sure your policies address new technologies.** Many sites I have reviewed don't have policies that touch on wireless. As technology changes, so must your policies.

- **When possible, don't allow laptops on your network.** While laptops are convenient, often they are not necessary. Because laptops bring a huge level of additional risk including viruses, lost data, and unlicensed software, they should only be permitted on a need-to-have basis.

If you are an employee who may have become a little creative in gaining access to the Internet on your company's network, I encourage you to stop. I realize that having complete access to the Internet is nice, but you could be putting your computer, your company's network, and even your job at risk. If you're the IT manager implementing the security restrictions, I encourage you to talk with the employees and find out what is needed and what can be blocked. Sometimes, giving just a little extra access may not increase network security risks. This, in turn, may be the difference between an employee working within the system rather than working against it.

TRUTH

35

Corporate laptop security

In 2005, there were more than 750,000 laptops stolen in the United State, up about 20% from the prior year. So it should come as no surprise when you hear about organizations that have reported lost or stolen data that these losses are often associated with lost or stolen laptops. On the other hand, maybe it should surprise you. One would think that with as much press as there has been regarding identity theft and lost data that companies would be doing far more to protect their data.

Let me first start with the obvious. On one of my conference trips, I went to lunch with some people who were also attending the same conference. When we got to the restaurant, I started to get out of the car with my backpack containing my laptop. I noticed one of the guys in my group was putting his backpack containing his laptop in the back seat. He asked if I wanted to leave my backpack behind since it would be a hassle to carry inside. I told him I would take mine. He just shrugged and laid his coat over the backpack. He climbed out of the car and closed the door, and we went into the restaurant.

This is not the first time I have seen someone do this, and when I talk to people about it, almost everyone admits they have done something similar. Now to step into reality: If you're a criminal who happens to be wandering around a parking lot looking for something interesting to steal, what do you think goes through your head when you look in the car with the coat lump? "Gee, nothing in this car but that big old coat. Obviously, I don't want to steal that, so I will move on." Maybe. However, I think that, like me, criminals are probably really thinking, "Gee, I wonder what's under that coat that was so important that the owner wanted to hide it. Think I'll take a little peek."

> Once confidential data is on the laptop in any form, it becomes a mobile time bomb.

So what makes laptops such a critical factor in dealing with identity theft? Simply put, they contain confidential information. Many people use laptops at work and at home. While at work, people are often interfacing with customer confidential information. Database files and confidential documents often end up residing on laptops. Sometimes the information is put there intentionally so that the employee can work on it from home. Other times the employee thinks he has deleted the files from the computer, not realizing that a hacker can easily restore the files, which actually haven't been deleted. Once confidential data is on the

One mistake by the employee, and suddenly you find your company entangled in a confidentiality nightmare.

laptop in any form, it becomes a mobile time bomb. One mistake by the employee, and suddenly you find your company entangled in a confidentiality nightmare.

A laptop doesn't have to be stolen to put the confidential information at risk. When the laptop is plugged in to your corporate network, it has been placed in what should be a secure environment. Your corporate firewall is keeping would-be hackers at bay. However, when employees go home and connect to the Internet through their home network, what security do *they* have?

Some Internet providers offer a limited level of protection, while others leave the security up to the user. In the latter, if that laptop has not been kept up to date with all the latest patches and the employee has not been trained on how to avoid malicious software, hackers can gain access to that laptop very quickly. The first response I receive when I explain this to people is, "I'm a nobody, so who is going to attack my computer?" Most of you probably realize by now that the majority of the home users whose computers have been compromised were not singled out. Instead, malicious software known as worms continuously attack random computers all over the world. It is just dumb luck if your computer is discovered by one of these worms.

As I said earlier, there are cases in which laptops are truly needed for business, and in those situations, there are several things you can do to keep confidential information protected while still gaining the benefits that a laptop provides.

- Require all laptops that access your network to maintain a certain level of security. Maintain patches, and ensure that a personal firewall is active on the laptop if it is used away from the office. Both Windows XP and Vista include built-in firewalls. (Though the Vista version is more robust.) While I feel every computer should have the personal firewall active, it should be absolutely mandatory with laptops.

- Install encryption software, such as Secure Boot, on every corporate laptop. This software requires that a username and strong password be entered at startup to decrypt the files on the drive. If the correct password isn't entered, all the files on the drive are inaccessible and useless. In rare cases, however, encryption software can become corrupted, so make sure you have a solid backup plan in place so that if an encrypted laptop becomes inaccessible, you can restore critical data.

- Install an encrypted partition if you can't encrypt the entire hard drive. There are a number of free products that will set up what looks like an additional hard drive on your computer. In reality, it simply takes a portion of your existing drive and sets it up as an encrypted drive. To access that drive, you must supply a pass phrase. Once you've accessed the drive, you can use it just like you would any other drive. Require your employees to place all confidential data into this partition.

- Train employees on the do's and don'ts of email attachments and malicious software. An employee needs to load only one malicious program onto his laptop while at home to put both his laptop and your network at risk.

- Don't allow laptops on your network if you have a choice.

While laptops may be able to increase productivity, they also increase your customers' risk of identity theft. Be certain you have done a complete risk assessment and understand that no matter what policies you implement, there is no sure thing when that laptop leaves your office.

TRUTH

36

Does your small business have a bull's-eye on it?

Have you ever thought about who holds your confidential information? Obviously, banks and other financial institutions come to mind, but who else? To be honest, I can't even come close to answering this question, because no one really knows. Hospitals, schools, law firms, insurance companies, accountants, and more keep your confidential information on file. The scary thing is that while banks and health care have strong government mandated regulations that are designed to pro-tect this information, many organizations have no guidelines at all.

I love my accountant. Recently, I visited her new office, which is located in a residential part of town that is slowly turning commercial. The office itself is a converted home and, while nice, I have to admit as I sat there that I couldn't help but think about security. In her computer sits my full name, social security number, job history, bank account number, as well as a slew of other random pieces of personal information. Is my data truly safe? I have no clue. I would like to think so, but then I have to assume that she is probably backing up her computer from time to time.

Where are those backup tapes being stored? At the office? At her home? And what about her computer? Does it have all the latest security patches? Is she aware of the types of email attacks that I have spoken about throughout this book? The question that I hate to think about even more is this: Will she even know if there has been a computer breach?

Obviously, if the front door of the building has been kicked in and the computer is gone, that should be a good indication. But what happens if an identity thief is able to hack into my accountant's computer and simply copy the data? My guess is that she may never have any idea. Why? Because she is an accountant, not an IT security professional. More importantly, she does not have a dedicated staff in place to monitor these types of attacks.

All that said, will I stop using my accountant? Of course not! She is great, and the fact is that her situation is not the exception, but the norm. There are thousands of accountants throughout the United States who are working in small offices—often home offices—where they are not only responsible for their own security, but the confidentiality of personal data for millions of people. In addition, while that insurance salesman who you work with to insure your home may work for a nationally recognized organization, odds are he is working out of his home or a small office. He, too, is responsible for maintaining the confidentially of your personal information. Again, you are left to wonder just how secure that data really is.

While there have been a large number of published cases involving accounting firms and insurance companies having confidential information stolen, these cases most often revolve around large organizations where the data was stolen from a laptop or directly from someone at a high level. It's rare that you hear anything about data stolen from a small mom-and-pop type accountant or insurance agent. Since it's unlikely that small businesses are more secure than the larger organizations, my fear is that these breaches may happen but go undetected or unreported.

While most states now require that confidential breaches be reported to the people affected, smaller incidents may still slip through the cracks.

If you own a business that maintains confidential information, which might include SSNs, credit card numbers, banking information, or other sensitive information, here are some precautions you should take to help ensure the integrity of your customers' private data.

> Since it's unlikely that small businesses are more secure than the larger organizations, my fear is that these breaches may happen but go undetected or unreported.

- Only ask for data you absolutely need. I still find organizations asking for information such as SSNs when they have absolutely no need for them. In fact, they are often illegally asking for this number.

- Use software that encrypts the data on your computer. Most new software stores all data in a format that cannot be read without a password.

- Make certain that your passwords are at least 10 characters, with mixed numbers and letters, and using at least one unique character, such as %, $, #, @, and so on. You can test the strength of any password at www.microsoft.com/protect/yourself/ password/checker.mspx.

- Use encrypted backup software if you make a backup of the data to digital archive tape (DAT). If you are not able to do this, store those backup tapes in a secure place, such as a safe or a safety deposit box at your bank. Taking them home and putting them in the closet is not secure. Treat these tapes like you would treat large amounts of cash.

- Make sure your computer has the latest patches available. Most operating systems allow you to automatically update them online. If you are not certain that your system is set up for this, contact someone who can help you. This is one of the most important security measures you can take.

- Ensure that you have a personal firewall installed on your computer. If you have Windows XP with Service Pack 2, make sure you have enabled the personal firewall that is available to you or that you have installed a third-party firewall. If you don't have Service Pack 2, get it. It's free and available on the Microsoft Web site. If you have Microsoft Vista, be certain your personal firewall is activated or that you have installed a third-party firewall.

- Beware of any new files or directories on your computer or copies of files that you did not make. This may be the only indication that you have had a breach. Contact someone who can investigate immediately. The sooner you respond to a potential issue, the greater chance you have of stopping it.

- Let your customers know if you have had a data breach. Doing nothing is often illegal and is putting the identity of every one of your customers at risk.

No matter how big or small your business, if you maintain confidential information, you have to take responsibility for ensuring it remains confidential.

While the majority of the attacks that happen today are focused on financial institutions, as those larger companies continue to tighten their security, identity thieves will continue to look elsewhere to acquire the data they need to commit their crimes.

TRUTH

My own identity theft experience

If you have never been a victim of identity theft, it might be hard to understand just how traumatic it is. You might think that because you're not on the hook for paying for fraudulent charges racked up by an identity thief, identity theft is not a big deal. The problem is that, while in theory, you aren't responsible for charges incurred by an identity thief, in reality, it's much more complicated. I know from personal experience.

About 10 years ago, I received a phone call from a collection agency. The woman I spoke with explained that her company was collecting on an unpaid phone bill. According to the caller, I failed to pay a rather large phone bill during a six-month span in an apartment in Chicago. In addition, the fees had been racked up more than two years earlier, and after the phone company had not been able to reach me to collect on the debt, this collection company had taken over. She was direct and authoritative. During her entire monologue, I sat quietly and just listened to everything. She ended by asking how I intended to pay the bill and listed a few options.

I asked what I thought was the obvious question, "So, does it matter that I have lived in California my entire life and never had an apartment in Chicago?" Her response indicated she didn't believe me. She asked me to verify the social security number, and I confirmed that it was mine. She then said, "Well, sir, it appears that you did open a phone account in Chicago."

It's been 10 years, but this conversation will be burned into my memory forever, as it was at this point that I first discovered that when it comes to identity theft, you are 100% guilty until proven innocent.

When it comes to identity theft, you are 100% guilty until proven innocent.

As we talked, I grew frustrated, and the collector became aggressive. Finally, she said she would be assigning me to another agent, and I could dispute the charges with this person.

A couple of days later, I received a call from another person who asked me to explain my side of the story again. I explained simply

148

that I was born in California and had lived in California my entire life. While I had visited Chicago a couple of times for business, I was certain I would have remembered living there for six months in an apartment. Again, the caller implied strongly that I might have forgotten that I lived in Chicago since it had been a couple of years ago. Finally, he gave me an address, to which I was to send copies of utility bills from the time period in question. While frustrated, I agreed.

In the meantime, I ran a credit report just to see what was happening. Sure enough, this phone bill was on my credit report showing that I was a deadbeat. I spent the next few weeks gathering copies of utility bills, which was no small task. After sending those copies, I went for nearly three weeks without hearing anything despite leaving repeated phone messages.

Finally, the collection agency called and said that the utility bills I sent were for the wrong months and that I needed to get copies of the bills from the previous month. Again, I spent several weeks tracking down copies of the bills they needed, and again, I didn't hear back from the collection agency for weeks. Then they called back and said the copies I had sent weren't legible. So, begrudgingly, I sent a third package of bills and again waited for a response that never came. After weeks went by, I called the company's main line and did reach someone who told me that my account had been handed off to another collection agency and that I needed to call them.

After multiple attempts to reach anyone at the second company and as I neared the one-year anniversary of this whole mess beginning, finally a real person gave me a new number to call and a new case number. When I called *that* number, it went to a voice mail system and again, I began leaving messages. Finally, when the second company called me back, I was told that I needed to send all the same bills I had sent to the first company. So I sent the bills again, along with a letter explaining the whole situation.

Weeks later, I received another call from the second collection agency saying that it hadn't received the copies of my bills, which I'd mailed to them. This time, the agency asked that I fax them. Two weeks later, I still could not verify that the agency had received my fax.

At this point, I started leaving several messages a day, and in another week or so, I received another call explaining that again the agency had not received my fax. This was about the moment that I swear I heard something in my head pop. I hung up the phone, wrote a short letter that simply read, "You will receive this fax every 15 minutes until I receive confirmation that you have it." I gave the papers to my receptionist and asked that she continue to send the 13 pages via fax to them every 15 minutes until I told her otherwise.

After several hours of faxing the same documents repeatedly, we received a fax that simply read, "We have received your fax. Please stop." While my identity theft issue was not over, I at least amused myself that day and felt that I could chalk one up for the little guy. It took another month before I received a call saying that my case had been cleared, another three months before I got something in writing, and another two months for me to contact all the credit bureaus and have the collection taken off my credit report.

In all, I spent almost two years working through the process, wasting untold time in the whole ordeal. I did manage to clean up my credit, but the process was absolutely ridiculous and, more importantly, it was clear from day one that I was the one on trial and was definitely guilty until proven innocent. What makes this story more ridiculous is the original phone bill that started this whole thing was for $600.00. That's right. It took two years and all that effort to resolve a single collection of less than $1,000. With my own experience fresh in my mind, I can only imagine the nightmare that many people have gone through when their identities have been stolen and a thief racks up thousands of dollars in debt.

TRUTH

38

It all started with a phone call

While the name of the person in this story has been changed, her story is true. Kathy Smith grew up in California, went to school in Houston, and settled down in a small town in Oklahoma. It isn't the kind of place where she worried about crime like she would in the big cities. Unfortunately for Kathy and millions of others throughout the United States, identity theft doesn't discriminate based on your zip code.

In April 2007, Kathy received a phone call from a cell phone carrier. The caller asked to speak with Kathy Jones. Kathy was a little confused at first since Jones was her maiden name. She explained that she was formerly Kathy Jones and asked what the call was regarding. The caller asked her if she had purchased a cell phone plan with a cell phone carrier in Houston, Texas. She told the caller that she had not set up an account with this company. The caller then read off the last four digits of her social security number and asked if it belonged to her. It did.

Identity theft doesn't discriminate based on your zip code.

The caller then explained that someone had purchased cellular service using her personal information. Also, while the thief paid the first few phone bills, the thief had stopped paying and the account was delinquent. Kathy made it clear that someone else had used her information. So she was transferred to the fraud department.

As the fraud department investigated the issue further, it was determined that the person using her information had given an incorrect birth date for Kathy. However, that mistake did not stop the thief from getting the original service agreement.

Since Kathy was not sure how to handle this type of crime, she was instructed by the cell carrier to contact the proper reporting agencies and file a fraud alert. While it is true that she needed to file a fraud alert, in reality she should have first gone to the police and filed an identity theft report. This omission came back to haunt Kathy later.

Kathy called the credit reporting agency and was walked through filing the fraud alert. Once she was done, she felt confident that she had addressed the matter and things would go back to normal. This is often what happens when people first become victims of identity theft. Most victims deal with the initial problem and assume that the issue has been resolved for good. Unfortunately, it generally is not that simple, and the first notification is only the starting point.

A few months later, Kathy started receiving credit card bills. Some of them were for credit cards using her maiden name, and others were for credit cards using a misspelled version of her current name. On average, the credit cards had a limit

Most victims deal with the initial problem and assume that the issue has been resolved for good. Unfortunately, it generally is not that simple.

of $1,000, and each one was maxed out. Of course, the person using the cards had failed to make any payments, and the card issuers had now tracked down the real Kathy under the assumption that she was evading payment.

After talking to the first credit card company and explaining that she had not opened the account, she was told that she needed to file a police report immediately. She would also need to fill out some forms, get them notarized, and then send everything back to the credit card company. The company also told her that she had a limited time in which to take care of the matter. Kathy filed the identity theft report with the police, had the forms notarized, and then sent them to the credit card company. She was now starting to understand how serious this really was.

After dealing with the first credit card company, she followed suit with the second, third, and fourth companies. Fighting this identity theft was becoming a full-time job for Kathy.

Finally, she started to feel as though she was getting control of her identity again. Because the credit cards had been issued before she had filed her fraud alert, she now thought she had shut the identity thief down. Unfortunately, the original fraud alert Kathy filed lasted for only 90 days. Of course, Kathy didn't know the fraud alert had expired, and sure enough, shortly after the fraud alert was lifted, the identity thief opened another credit card.

Unfortunately, no one told Kathy that filing the proper identity theft report with the police entitled her to receive a free seven-year fraud alert and a free credit freeze. In fact, until I was interviewing her for this story, she had never even heard of these options.

Later, Kathy was forced to deal with some inheritance issues stemming from her father's declining health. While she was working through these issues, she attempted to open a new banking account only to discover that her name no longer matched the name associated with her social security number. No matter what she said or how much she protested, the bank refused to allow her to open an account.

I would like to say that this story has a happy ending. However, at the time of this writing, Kathy still had not resolved all her identity theft issues. She has yet to find out why her name no longer matches her number, and she continues to try to undo all the damage done to her credit.

My fear is that the identity thief is still on the loose and continuing to attack her identity. Kathy did pull a recent credit report and found many disturbing additions, including several different residences under many different aliases. These names are all similar to her real name, just slightly misspelled. She assumes that the person using her identification has somehow learned of her real name, possibly while talking to a debt collector, and is using information to continue attacking her identity.

Dealing with identity theft is something Kathy can do only in her spare time. Like many of us, she cannot just drop everything and focus all her attention on identity theft. In addition, before I spoke to Kathy, she had no idea what all her options were and what she could do to help protect herself and restore her identity. And that is the underlying problem. While everyone is talking about identity theft, most people don't know what to do after they have become the next identity theft statistic. We'll delve into these issues next.

TRUTH

39

Stopping thieves in their tracks

When it comes to protecting one's identity, most people have no clue where to start. While there are no silver bullets to guarantee your safety from identity thieves, following the advice I provide here can make a huge difference. I focus on what to do if you think someone may have gained access to your confidential information and how to stay one step ahead of a would-be identity thief.

Fraud alerts

One of the first steps you should take when trying to protect your identity is to set up a fraud alert. There are two types of fraud alerts:

> When it comes to protecting one's identity, most people have no clue where to start.

- **Initial fraud alert**—You can place an initial fraud alert if you suspect you have been or are about to become a victim of identity theft. In my opinion, everyone falls under the category of "about to become a victim." You should file for an initial fraud alert if you think your identity might be compromised. This type of alert is active for 90 days. During this time, creditors that follow "reasonable policies and procedures" as outlined by federal law will refuse to open a new account. Unfortunately, since "reasonable policies and procedures" is a loose term, credit can still be given to identity thieves using accounts under fraud alert.

- **Extended fraud alert**—If you are already a victim of identity theft and provide one of the credit report agencies with your identity theft report, you are eligible for the extended fraud alert. The extended fraud alert stays on your credit report for seven years. During this time, creditors are required to speak with you or meet with you before issuing any credit under your name. In addition, your name is automatically removed from all marketing lists and preapproved credit offers for five years. Even with this type of fraud alert, some identity thieves have been able to slip through the cracks and receive credit approval. It's still worth the effort to file this alert.

Everyone is entitled to one free credit report from each of the three credit reporting agencies in a 12-month period. However, if you file for an extended fraud alert, you are entitled to two free credit reports from each of the three credit reporting agencies during a 12-month period. Regardless of whether you get all the reports, I recommend that you get them on a staggered schedule. For example, if you get only one per agency, get one, wait four months, and then request another from the second agency. Wait four more months, and then request another from the third agency. This gives you far greater coverage over the year.

Filing is free, and you are only required to file for a fraud alert at one of the three reporting agencies. (The three reporting agencies are Equifax, Experian, and TransUnion. See the section " Credit reporting agencies" at the end of Truth 46 for their complete contact information.) Once you've filed, the agency that you file with passes the information to the remaining two at no charge to you.

Identity theft report

Many people are not aware of the identity theft report. This is a police report designed specifically for identity theft victims. One of the most important steps you can take if you have become an identity theft victim is to fill out this report. This report details everything that you are aware of and is required by many creditors and businesses that you are dealing with when cleaning up your credit. However, simply filing a general police report is not enough. You must also file the identity theft report. Because this type of filing is different from other police reports, it is important that you file in person. If you file over the phone or via the Internet, getting the identity theft report is far more difficult. If you have already filed a police report but not an identity theft report with the police, contact the Federal Trade Commission (www.ftc.gov).

Credit/security freeze

In 2007, the reporting agencies began offering *credit or security freezes.* A freeze is different from a fraud alert. If you have been the victim of identity theft, you can set up a freeze at no charge. However, unlike fraud alerts, you must file for a freeze at each of the reporting agencies. If you have *not* been a victim of identity theft, each reporting agency charges a fee if you want to activate a freeze.

A security freeze means that the reporting agency blocks anyone from getting a copy of your credit report without your permission. You are provided with a PIN or password that is required to release the credit report. A freeze generally is more secure than a fraud alert, and the two combined are a great defense against the majority of identity theft attacks. Lifting a freeze can take between 3 to 30 days, and you must contact each reporting agency separately.

Stop preapproved credit offers

Reporting agencies sell your information to advertisers who, in turn, use that information to send you preapproved credit card offers. You can stop most of them from ever being sent by going to the Web site www.optoutprescreen.com and filling out the form. You can choose to opt out permanently or for a five-year period. In addition, once you have opted out, you can always go back to the site if you decide to opt back in. If you do not want to use the form online, you also have the option of calling a toll-free number at 1-888-5OPT-OUT (1-888-567-8688). You can also get on the "do not call" list to stop telemarketers from calling you: www.donotcall.gov.

40

Installing proper identity theft protection

Check your email on any given day, and the probability that you have received potentially malicious emails is quite high. Unfortunately, there is no real solution to these unwanted emails and, more importantly, there does not seem to be any slowdown in these types of attacks. Many home users have no idea that their personal computers remain under constant attack via their connection to the Internet. These attacks range from worms that continue to self-propagate over the Internet to malicious Web sites that are designed to attack your computer when you browse them. While a secured computer will not end your risks of identity theft, it is a key component in your arsenal against would-be attackers.

Personal firewalls

New operating systems, such as Windows XP Service Pack 2 or Vista and Macintosh OS X, include built-in firewalls. The problem is that most people who have the ability to run the personal firewall either choose not to enable it, have it misconfigured or, even worse, simply don't pay attention to the warnings that those firewalls give them.

The personal firewall is designed to serve many purposes. One of the most important functions is the capability to block external connections from accessing your computer. Hackers use a variety of methods to scan for unsecured computers connected to the Internet and then have an arsenal of weapons they can use to assault any vulnerable system they find. Unfortunately, for the typical user, these vulnerabilities aren't visible and, worse still, it's not usually apparent when you have been attacked. Once a hacker gains access to your computer, he might scan it, looking for personal information he can use to steal your identity, or he might enslave your computer to use its horsepower in attacks on other computers. Or the hacker might install viruses designed to wreak havoc. Whatever his intent, blocking hackers is job number one if you have a computer connected to the Internet.

The personal firewall is designed to watch your back, blocking access to your computer and requests sent from your computer unless you specifically allow it. With a firewall in place, many hacking attempts are thwarted simply by the fact that the firewall makes your computer invisible to the rest of the Internet.

Unfortunately, this protection does come at a nominal price—pop-up messages alerting you to activity coming in or going out to the Internet. These alerts can be annoying until you have trained your firewall on which programs have carte blanch to run without permission and which need to ask each time. Sadly, these alerts lead some users to either disable the firewall or blindly okay each alert from the firewall.

If your operating system does not include a built-in firewall, I strongly suggest that you look at purchasing a firewall application immediately. There are a variety of firewalls from security giants Norton and McAfee as well as a number of free firewalls available for download.

Antivirus software

While most new computers come with some level of antivirus protection, most of these services require an annual subscription to continue providing protection. Like personal firewalls, there are free versions of antivirus protection available for download from the Internet. While I prefer one of the major retail products, if you are on a limited budget, the free antivirus solutions do suffice. Make sure that you set up your antivirus program to receive automatic updates.

> Having frequently updated antivirus software is no longer a luxury; it is an absolute necessity.

The bottom line is that having frequently updated antivirus software is no longer a luxury; it is an absolute necessity. Without it, the question is not if your computer will get a virus, but when.

Encryption

The success of wireless networking has made the laptop more portable than ever before. I have not had a desktop computer in about five years and can't even imagine going back to one.

The problem, however, is while your desktop computer sits at home or in your office protected behind locked doors, your laptop is on the move. It's with you in the car, on the plane, or sitting next to you as you ride the subway. Gone are the locked doors and the security that came with desktop PCs. Now *you* are the only protection that your computer has and, in turn, the only protection for the confidential information that resides on it.

So what happens when someone steals your laptop? Well, that all depends on whether the files on your computer are encrypted. Encryption programs are designed to make data unreadable without a security key. While there are a number of expensive solutions that can encrypt your computer's entire hard drive, there are also a number of free solutions that you can use and still have the security you need.

While I generally try not to mention products by name, both TrueCrypt and Cryptainer Lite offer the capability to create encrypted drives on your existing computer and, more importantly, they are both free of charge. Once you've installed the product, simply place your confidential files into the newly created system folder. When you log back in, this folder will be locked and unable to be accessed without the security key. Therefore, if someone were to steal your computer, the data in this folder would be relatively safe.

Obviously, encryption is not going to be for everyone. If you are just lucky to be able to pick up your email, you might not want to mess with this technology. However, if you are using your laptop at the office and then taking it home with you, I would suggest you look into securing any potentially confidential information. Also, while I have focused on laptops due to their obvious risks, encryption is valuable on desktops, too, since it does help protect you from hackers and identity thieves.

TRUTH

41

When a free credit report isn't free

With identity theft being such a hot topic these days, it's no doubt that you have seen the commercials, heard the radio ads, or seen the Web page banners offering free credit reports. In fact, you've probably thought seriously about getting a free credit report, especially if you have been reading along in this book about the horrors a dedicated identity thief can inflict upon you. Just know that much like most things in life, "free" things usually have strings attached.

When "free" actually means "monthly charge"

After hearing all the media hoopla about identity theft, you decide to visit a free credit report site. After searching for "free credit report" in Google, you come across a professional-looking Web page offering a free credit report. The form prompts you for your name, address, phone number, and email address. Next, the site requests your social security number, date of birth, and credit card information. But you just finished reading *The Truth About Identity Theft*, and you are no fool. So you check to make sure you are at a legitimate site. You verify with the Better Business Bureau that the company is legitimate and notice it has several certificates on its Web site that do track back to prove it actually is who it says it is. Satisfied, you go back to the Web site and continue.

> You didn't actually get a free credit report. What you got was a credit monitoring service that gives out a free credit report with purchase.

You do notice that the right side of the screen shows a checkout statement. You look closer and see that the itemized list includes a free credit report, free credit score, free credit monitoring, online delivery, and 24/7 access to your report, all free. After entering all your confidential information, you are asked to read and approve a license agreement. You quickly scroll through it, but at 460 lines, you would need to be an attorney to have a clue what it means.

You complete the form, and within a few minutes you have your credit report. A month or two passes, and you notice a strange charge of $12.99 appearing on your credit card statement. After some searching, you discover that the company that provided your free credit report has just charged you $12.99. So you visit the site again and reread the license agreement. You notice that in small print, the company told you that by getting this free credit report, you are signing up for a free 30-day enrollment in its credit watch program. After the 30 days, you will be charged $12.99 a month to continue the service. Further, the license agreement states the following:

> "You may cancel your Credit Monitoring membership at any time during the trial period without charge. If you wish to continue your membership in Credit Monitoring beyond the trial period, do nothing and your membership will automatically continue without interruption. The monthly fee (plus sales tax, if applicable) will be charged to your credit card account at the conclusion of the trial period and your membership will continue automatically, billable monthly at the prevailing rate."

Sure enough, you didn't actually get a free credit report. What you got was a credit monitoring service that gives out a free credit report with purchase. Technically speaking, the company did nothing wrong. Sure, it was easy to be misled, but had you read all the fine print, you could have caught on to what was happening. Don't feel bad, though. You're not alone. At www.ripoffreport.com, there are hundreds of complaints from people who have fallen for similar offers.

There is some good news. You can get free credit reports online from a site that is sponsored by the three reporting agencies. In fact, under federal law, you have the right to receive one free credit report from each of the three agencies every 12 months. Visit www.annualcreditreport.com. If you are not able to go online or are uncomfortable submitting your confidential information online, you may also request your report via the phone at 1-877-322-8228.

While you are allowed to request all three reports at the same time, I recommend that you stagger the requests so that you receive a different report each four months so that your reports will span the entire year.

Identity theft protection

While monitoring your credit is important, many people have decided that they would rather pay an organization to protect their identity than do it themselves. You may have seen the commercials where the CEO of one of these identity theft protection companies gives out his social security number on national television and explains that he doesn't have to worry because he uses its service. It's a convincing ad. So what it is doing to protect your identity that allows the CEO to be so confident that he is willing to give out his social security number?

All these companies are doing for you is setting an automatic 90-day fraud alert and then renewing it every 90 days. They also remove you from mailing lists and order free credit reports in your behalf. All that is helpful, but you can do those things yourself. The only thing most of these companies offer that you can't do for yourself is providing identity theft insurance coverage. Check with your insurance agent, however, to see if your homeowner's insurance offers identity theft coverage at a fraction of the cost.

If you are busy, have the expendable income, and are willing to pay for the convenience, using one of these services will definitely keep you more secure than doing nothing. If you think you can remember to fill out a form once every 90 days, request your credit reports every four months, and your homeowner's insurance provider can cover you for far less, I would suggest not spending your money for professional identity theft protection.

In the end, it all comes down to doing something. Don't just wait until something is done to you.

TRUTH

42

Getting your life back in order

Getting your life back in order after an identity theft is far easier said than done. One of the main reasons these thieves are so successful is because people often don't know what to do after the attack or how to ward off the thief who has compromised their identity. Following is a list of things you should do if your identity has been stolen.

- Don't panic. Finding out that a thief has charged purchases in your name is alarming. However, getting upset, arguing with the collection agency, or freaking out will not solve anything. Instead, document everything you do, everyone you talk to, and anything you are asked to do.

> Getting upset, arguing with the collection agency, or freaking out will not solve anything.

- Contact the company that sent you the bill. Make it clear that you did not incur these charges and that you want to speak with someone who deals with fraudulent accounts. Note the names of anyone you speak to, and write down everything that is discussed. Most likely, the company will ask for a copy of an identity theft police report. (See Truth 39, "Stopping thieves in their tracks.")

- If you have found that there are fraudulent checks being written against your checking account, contact your bank and put a stop payment on all outstanding checks. Don't attempt to selectively stop some checks while letting others go through. You can't be sure how the thief is drafting checks from your account, and it's possible that the thief has printed his own checks. It's better to stop all checks, change your account number, and get new checks.

  Also, ask your bank to write a letter that you can supply to anyone who received one of your canceled checks. Generally, most creditors will waive fees for canceled checks if you are the victim of identity theft. Your bank might ask you to file a claim with its fraud department, and eventually you should be able to recover money stolen from your account.

- If a debt collector calls you regarding a bill that is fraudulent, make it clear that you did not incur this bill. Ask for complete contact information for the collection agency. Also, ask for whom they are collecting the debt, including company name, phone number, address, and total amount due. Ask what they need from you to clear this up. Lastly, make it clear that you do not intend to pay the bill.

  Some collectors are aggressive. Don't get abusive. Make it clear that the charges aren't yours and that you want to file a fraud claim. Note that some scam artists will actually pose as an agent from a collection agency in an attempt to collect money from you. Often, they will start with a higher number and then offer to take a lower number if you pay over the phone. Don't fall for this ruse.

- Request a free credit report from one of the three reporting agencies. (See Truth 41, "When a free credit report isn't free.") It can take a few months before items make it to your credit history. If you do see suspicious activity, contact each of the companies listed on your report. Getting a credit report right away will be useful since you will need it when you make your police report.

- Go to the local police and file an identity theft report. Some departments might allow you to file via the phone or online, but I suggest that you file the report in person. It is important that you file an identity theft report, not just a standard police report. This report will contain the names of any organizations that you are aware of where there was fraudulent activity.

- File a credit freeze with each of the three reporting agencies. (See Truth 39, "Stopping thieves in their tracks.") A credit freeze should stop any business from being able to pull your credit report or open new credit with your social security number without your approval.

- Request an extended fraud alert from one of the three reporting agencies. (See Truth 39.) If you have an identity theft report from the police, you can file an extended alert, which lasts seven years. Without the report, you can file only an initial alert, which lasts 90 days.

- Contact every organization at which you believe there has been fraudulent activity using your personal information. Be sure to document who you spoke with and what damage has been done, and try to discover if the organization has already reported issues to the credit reporting agencies. By law, once an organization has been notified that you are dealing with identity theft, it is not allowed to make claims to reporting agencies. So the sooner you can let an organization know what's going on, the easier it will be to clean up your credit.

- Expect each creditor to require information from you. Generally, the affidavit that the FTC makes available is accepted by creditors. You can download it from www.ftc.gov/bcp/conline/pubs/credit/affidavit.pdf. You should also ask creditors to send you something in writing acknowledging that they are aware you are dealing with identity theft so that you have something for your records. You must also ask them to send you and your local law enforcement a copy of any documents that relate to this issue, which may include transaction records. This is something that creditors must supply you by federal law.

- Follow up with any correspondence that you had with these organizations in written form. The letter should include a summary of the conversation between you and that organization. Be sure to document what each company asked you to do and your understanding of how the issue will be resolved. Send the letter via certified mail.

- Contact every organization where you have a credit card or banking account. Request to add a unique password to these accounts, which most creditor and banks will allow you to do. Make sure that you remember the password since you will need it when you call in to get any information on the accounts. If it turns out there are issues, be sure to speak to someone in the fraud department, and then follow up with a written letter explaining the issue.

- As organizations begin to cancel the fraudulent charges, be sure to have them send you a written statement showing that you do not owe the debt and that the account was closed. In addition, ask if they will be notifying the reporting agencies or if they had placed a claim on your record. While I have found they will say "yes," often they never actually do it. Once organizations agree that the amounts are not due, you can also contact the reporting agencies and file a dispute to have the claims removed.

In this country, your credit is your life and it's up to you to fight for your name.

Cleaning up your name and credit history takes time. You have to go in circles with some agencies, while others handle things quickly and professionally. The good news is that you are not the first one who has notified the credit company or collection agency that you are a victim of identity theft. By now, every organization is not only aware of it but generally has specific policies and guidelines already in place for what you need to do. While some of them do not make it easy, it is important that you do not give up. In this country, your credit is your life, and it's up to you to fight for your name.

TRUTH

43

Somebody's watching me

By now, you most certainly have heard the term spyware and might even know a little about it. But did you know that, in addition to showing you ads you didn't want to see and collecting marketing information about your Web surfing habits, some spyware is malicious and identity thieves can use it to harvest your every keystroke, including your name, credit card numbers, and any other personally identifying information you type?

There are three main types of spyware.

> The biggest problem with spyware is that most users install it without even knowing.

- **Information gatherer**—This type simply runs in the background on your computer tracking your Web-browsing habits. Every site you visit is logged, and that information is relayed back to a master site on the Internet. This is all done transparently and, with the exception of slowing down your computer, most people never have any idea it is happening. In the "legal" version, this software should not transmit confidential information.

- **Ad generator**—This monitors every site that you visit and generates pop-up ads when you visit certain sites. For example, if you visit a site selling gardening tools, the software might generate a pop-up for another site selling gardening tools. Most of the time users just assume the pop-up was generated by the Web page they were visiting and don't realize it was really created by this spyware. In other cases, this software actually modifies Web pages as they are being displayed. When this happens, words throughout the Web page start becoming hyperlinks to other pages. For example, if the word *tools* is found in the text on the Web page, it now becomes a link that, when clicked, takes you to another site that sells tools.

- **Malicious spyware**—While most spyware is annoying, this type is truly dangerous. This software is designed to capture your every keystroke. So when you visit an online banking application, the username and password that you type in are recorded. Or when you enter a credit card number to pay for a purchase online, that information is being recorded. Then that data is automatically transferred from your computer to a master site waiting to receive the data. This collection and transfer happens without your knowledge. Also, this type of software might search your hard drive looking for files known to contain confidential information and might even steal cookies from your computer, which contain personal information.

The biggest problem with spyware is that most users install it without even knowing. In Internet Explorer 6, when you visit a Web site that attempts to send you a software script known as ActiveX, you receive a security warning that tells you the site is attempting to install and run an ActiveX script and asks if you want to let it run. Often the developers of the spyware code it so that, instead of listing the name of the script being listed in the warning dialog box, they create a warning that reads something like this: "This program will allow you to visit this site securely; select Yes now to continue." Most people agree to run the code without realizing they are giving permission to install software that might contain spyware. Users who are more paranoid may select No. In that case, the site has been designed to go into a loop bringing the user directly back to the security warning again. Each time the user selects No, the site just tries again. Because people can't get out of the loop, they generally give up and finally select Yes. If you find yourself stuck in one of these loops, press the Esc key on your keyboard over and over while you click the No button on the screen to stop the loop.

In many cases, spyware is bundled with free software that you can download. Screen savers and peer-to-peer file-sharing programs often contain spyware. In fact, when it comes to screen savers, it's rare that one doesn't contain some type of spyware. And many times the spyware is truly malicious.

When it comes to peer-to-peer file sharing, there is often a level of deception that takes place. One of the most popular applications has a notice on the Web site that says, "No Spyware." You might think this notice means they do not put spyware on your computer. In reality, however, if you read the fine print, you see that a number of programs are being placed on your computer that are defined by most as spyware. While I will give the application credit for listing what is being installed in the license agreement, it is still deceptive to the end user.

So what can you do to avoid spyware?

■ Whenever a Web site prompts you with a security warning to install and run software, you should always select not to install it unless you are absolutely certain what the software is doing. *"No" should be your default answer for everything.*

■ While some free software can be useful, much of the free software on the Internet is dangerous. It could contain malicious code, which might put your confidentiality at risk. If you are not certain about the software you are downloading, it is best to err on the side of caution and choose not to install it.

■ Now that I have turned you off of free software, let me tell you about two free applications that are truly great for removing spyware (although Microsoft does provide a free spyware blocking program—Windows Defender).

Spybot Search & Destroy—Searches through your computer, notifies you, and removes just about all potential spyware. It is highly recommended that you read the user manual before attempting to run this software. (www.safer-networking.org.)

Ad-Aware 2008 Free—Searches through your computer, notifies you, and removes all potential spyware. (www.lavasoft.com/products/ad_aware_free.php.)

44

Wireless security at home

About four months ago, I moved into a new home. At the time that my wife and I were looking, we thought we were asking all the right questions. It seemed like a great location, it was the perfect size, and it even had a pool. Since I work from home, I thought it would probably be a good idea to get my high-speed Internet turned on. Sure, I should have planned ahead, but I figured as much as I travel, the ISP would get it installed while I was on the road. Imagine my surprise when I discovered that my home was located in a "dead zone," which basically meant I couldn't get wireless access. In the meantime, my work was piling up, and the lack of Internet access was causing a problem.

While most people would have bitten the bullet and gone with a dial-up, I had another idea. I got out my power converter that allows me to power my laptop using the cigarette lighter in my car, and I hit the road. With my laptop beside me, I started to cruise the neighborhood. It turns out that only my street is "dead." Ridiculous as it may seem, it's true. For me, this had a silver lining, since as soon as I hit the next street over, my laptop started showing numerous available wireless connections that were broadcasting from my new neighbors' homes. This would be my salvation.

When you install a wireless device in your home, it affords you the ability to use your laptop from any room in the house without the need for an Ethernet cable. This ease of mobility is great, but it often comes at the detriment of the user. You see, by default when you install this type of device, it is open to the world. This means if some guy happens to be driving down your street with his laptop in his car, he can simply connect to your wireless device and begin using your Internet service—for example, someone who lived in a "dead zone" and did not have high-speed Internet access of his own.

For the next several weeks, I found dozens of locations near my home where the sun was blocked by trees, so I didn't bake in my car and didn't look too suspicious sitting there all day long. I had full-speed Internet, and no one was any the wiser. Ultimately, I ended up installing DSL at home, but my few weeks working out of my car gave me a scary look at just how vulnerable many of my neighbors were.

Some might think I was breaking the law, but was I really? Often, hotels offer free wireless service in their rooms. Many coffee shops and book stores offer wireless access for free as well. How do you connect? The same way that I connected to my neighbors' wireless. You simply open your computer, search for networks in range, and choose an unsecured access point. I didn't crack any passwords, and I certainly didn't receive any notices announcing that I was not authorized to access the service. So for all I know, these people had placed these wireless devices out there just for people like me who were in need of quick access to the Internet. I mean, why else would they not have put a password on the device?

Obviously, these wireless devices should have been secured properly, but not because of a potential freeloader like myself. The risks to home users who leave their wireless access points open is much greater. When I am hired to break into a company, often I go after computers by using an open wireless access point I find on the company network. The same can be done with home users. What most people don't realize is that once I am on your network via the wireless device, I can start monitoring all the traffic on your network. If you receive an email, I see it. too. An instant message? I'm watching. You browse to your favorite Web sites, and I see everything you see. And that's just the beginning.

> When I am hired to break into a company, often I go after computers by using an open wireless access point that I find on the company network.

Often, your Internet service provider (ISP) offers you an added level of security by blocking all incoming traffic to your computer. This "firewall" protects you from the would-be hackers of the world. So even if you have done a poor job of securing your computer, it's okay because your ISP has you covered.

Now if I gain access via your wireless device, I have bypassed the ISP's external security, and I am sitting right next to your computer on your network. If you have any vulnerability, I can find it in minutes. The next thing you know, I am perusing files on your system, recording even more information about where you're browsing, and most importantly, if you're doing anything from online banking to e-commerce. Basically, it takes no time at all for me to gather all your account information, and just like that, the identity theft begins.

Of course, it's not always that easy, and there are certain things that you can and should do to protect your computer and your identity.

- Add a password to your wireless device. Each device is different, so you need to read the instructions to find out how to do that on yours. You need to make sure your password is difficult to crack. Using a single word won't do. It needs to be a large password, and it should be random letters (upper- and lowercase), numbers, and symbols.

- Make sure your device supports Wi-Fi protected access (WPA) and that you chose that type of encryption. There are two forms: WEP and WPA. Through the years, wired equivalent privacy (WEP) has been hacked numerous times, to the point where now it is no more secure than a closed window on your house when the burglar is carrying a lead pipe. If your wireless device offers only WEP, you should probably consider purchasing a newer device.

Wired equivalent privacy (WEP) has been hacked numerous times, to the point where now it is no more secure than a closed window on your house when the burglar is carrying a lead pipe.

- Don't leave confidential information on your computer. I have broken into hundreds of computers that contained everything from text files that held lists of passwords to files that held all the user's credit card numbers and expiration dates. If you are going to keep this kind of information on your desktop, you must encrypt these files. If you don't, you are just asking for trouble.

45

Crack-proofing your passwords

My three-year-old son likes to play a game with me that he calls What's the Password? This game consists of him standing in a doorway with his arms stretched out to block access through it. He then asks me for the password, and if I get it correct, I am allowed to pass. I am, of course, expected to want to go through this same door dozens of times in a row, each time being forced to answer the challenge. To date, there is still only one correct response that he will accept to open the gate. That word is password.

At first I found this funny and played along. However, it has been going on for a couple of months now, and quite honestly, I am starting to get a little concerned. What if my son ends up to be one of those kinds of people? You know the types—the ones who use *qwerty*, *asdfgh*, and *password* as their password. What if, instead of following the password guidelines of alphanumeric, upper- and lowercase with a minimum of eight characters, my son is one of those people whose password is simply his name backward. Or what if he uses the password *admin* for the admin account or *toor* for the root password?

Over the past several years, I have run across these passwords, or others that are just as bad, at one customer site or another. Often, I have found them just by taking a stab in the dark, even without a password-cracking tool. And now it seems my son is on this same destructive path of becoming a password degenerate. Passwords have always been the strong and weak point of security. Strong passwords generally indicate stronger security, while weak passwords lead to system compromise. So why do passwords fail to protect so many users and organizations? To answer that, you have to look at a much bigger picture.

Poorly designed passwords

When a password is created without the help of an automated tool, most people choose things that are easy to remember. Sometimes it's the first letter of several words. In other cases, people use dates, such as an anniversary or birth date. Though these can be used in a way to create a solid password, more times than not, these creations are done incorrectly. A person's name with a date at the end, such as Jim1970, will be found by almost every password cracker in existence.

The password January1970 is equally bad. A simple, yet effective, way to find out just how easy it is to crack a password is to download a program called LOphtCrack. A quick Google search on the Internet can give you several links to the software. This program looks through your Windows password registry and cracks the passwords, generally in minutes. In addition, this program can monitor the network and pick up NT passwords off the wire.

To be fair, this program does take advantage of some issues with Microsoft's security. But a strong password can hold its own for a long time against such a program.

Brute-force crackers

Brute-force crackers generally come in two designs. The first is based on word lists. These lists contain thousands of words that an automated program attempts to use against an account. UNIX systems and routers are generally most vulnerable to these types of attacks since most do not lock out an account after a set number of failed attempts. The cracker just keeps sending over word after word to use as the password until the program lets it in. These complete lists have many variations of the same word, such as root and r00t. By changing letters such as *O* with the number zero or *l* with the number one, often people think they are being crafty. Though these tricks may work in some cases to protect you, they are not recommended.

The second type of brute-force software is based on an algorithm. If a hacker has all the time in the world, this is generally guaranteed to work. The automated program simply tries every letter combination until it finds the correct match. For example, if the program has been set up to know that the minimum password length is three, it starts out with *aaa*. It then submits *aab*, then *aac*, and so on, and so on. Again, this is time-consuming, and these crackers can be complex and capable of using hundreds of computers at the same time to run the cracks.

If a hacker is performing this kind of attack against a static password on your server, he will eventually gain access. Of course, in that case, one would hope you have some sort of security in place to monitor the total number of failed attempts to log in. But that's a whole other matter.

With this type of attack, bigger is generally better. Minimum password length becomes an important part of the equation. Obviously, eight characters instead of five characters requires hundreds of thousands of additional attempts and reduces the likelihood the password will be cracked.

Put old passwords out to pasture

Once people find the perfect password, the next problem is letting go. Simply put, you need to change passwords periodically. I have read policies in corporations that range from 30 days to 6 months. I like the 90- to 120-day range. Yes, I know it's hard to remember new passwords, and I am the first to admit I have broken this rule on more than one occasion. However, if you are looking for a truly secure environment, this strategy should be mandatory. By the way, bouncing between two passwords over and over is not changing your password. It's a sly loophole, but you are only putting yourself and your organization at risk.

One suggestion I have is to change portions of your current password. By using four of the original characters and changing the other four, you increase your chances of remembering the password while still changing it enough to be secure. Then, for the next change, remove something from the password that had still been part of the previous password. Over time, your entire password changes, while you are only required to remember four new characters each time.

Any attack that requires a large amount of resources puts a hacker at risk of being caught.

Even though most any password can be cracked if the thief puts enough time into it, any attack that requires a large amount of resources puts a hacker at risk of being caught and can set off alarms on the network.

TRUTH

46

Who you gonna call?

Many of these contact addresses and numbers appear throughout this book. However, if you are ever a victim of identity theft, it will be handy to have them all in one place. Of course, if there is a Web address listed, you most certainly should check there for downloadable forms and reports that you will need.

Credit reporting agencies

- Equifax
  1-800-525-6285
  www.equifax.com
  P.O. Box 740241
  Atlanta, GA 30374-0241

- Experian
  1-888-EXPERIAN (397-3742)
  www.experian.com
  P.O. Box 2002
  Allen, TX 75013

- TransUnion
  1-800-680-7289
  www.transunion.com
  Fraud Victim Assistance Division
  P.O. Box 6790
  Fullerton, CA 92834-6790

Free credit reports (free with no strings)

- www.annualcreditreport.com

Filing a complaint with the Federal Trade Commission (FTC)

- 1-877-ID-THEFT (438-4338);
  Identity Theft Clearinghouse, Federal Trade Commission
  600 Pennsylvania Avenue
  NW, Washington, DC 20580
  www.ftc.gov/bcp/edu/microsites/idtheft/consumers/
  filing-a-report.html

Locate your state attorney general

From time to time, a local police department may not be willing to take an identity theft police report. In these cases, you should contact your state attorney general to find out the laws. In most cases, this person can provide you with assistance in moving forward with resolving your identity theft issues.

- www.naag.org/attorneys_general.php

Links dedicated to identity theft

- Stickley on Security
  www.stickleyonsecurity.com

- Federal Trade Commission (FTC)
  www.ftc.gov/bcp/edu/microsites/idtheft/consumers/defend.html

- Internal Revenue Service (IRS)
  www.irs.gov/individuals/article/0,,id=136324,00.html

- U.S. Department of Justice
  www.usdoj.gov/criminal/fraud/websites/idtheft.html

- Department of the Treasury
  www.treas.gov/offices/domestic-finance/financial-institution/cip/
  identity-theft.shtml

- Better Business Bureau
  www.bbbonline.org/IDTheft/index.asp

- Social Security Online
  www.ssa.gov/pubs/10064.html

- FBI Fraud Complaint Center
  www.ic3.gov

Opt-out lists

- Pre-approved offers from the credit reporting agencies
  888-567-8688
  www.optoutprescreen.com

- Telemarketing lists
  (888) 382-1222
  www.donotcall.gov

- Mail marketing lists
  www.dmaconsumers.org/cgi/offmailinglist

Acknowledgments

Writing a book turned out to be a lot more work than I imagined. So to my wife, who continued to wish me encouragement when I slowed down, I say thank you. To my sons, who I see far too little of while I am on the road: I love you and I will be home soon. To Tina Davis: I owe a huge thank-you to you for reading every word I wrote and for making this book look like I had a grasp of the English language. To Renee Cragun: Thanks for putting up with the weekend calls and giving me greatly needed advice. To my editor, Rick Kughen: Thank you for your help and patience.

To my original business partners, Pete Stewart and Rob Guba: I am truly lucky to have worked with both of you and thank you both for everything. Tracey, thank you for being a sounding board to my many absurd ideas. To Joe, Brian, Dayle, and basically the entire TraceSecurity engineering team: It should be clear that without all of you, there would be no TraceSecurity. To Jon Keyler: You taught me there is more to life than a computer. To my sister, Jenney: I'm sure you wish to thank me for being such a terrific brother. To my Mom and Dad: You've been the yin and yang of my life. Without both of you being so different, I would not be the person I am today. Thank you for everything!

About the Author

Jim Stickley is CTO and Vice President of Strategic Operations at TraceSecurity Inc. He was one of the original founders of TraceSecurity and is a renowned security expert. He has been involved in thousands of security services for financial institutions, Fortune 100 corporations, health care facilities, legal firms, insurance companies, and government agencies. He has been a security consultant for numerous magazines and newspapers, and he has been featured in *Time Magazine*, *Business Week*, *Fortune Magazine*, *The New York Times*, and many other industry-specific publications such as *PC Magazine* and *Security Focus*. He also has been showcased on NBC's *Nightly News*, CNN's *NewsNight*, several CNBC programs including *The Big Idea* and Business Nation, and numerous times on NBC's *Today Show*. He has physically breached the security of more than 1,000 facilities nationwide and had access to billions of dollars through stolen identities. When not on assignment, Jim continues to serve as a speaker and has delivered hundreds of speeches at security-related trade shows, conventions, seminars, and forums throughout the U.S. and other countries, covering topics ranging from identity theft to national cyberterrorism. Be sure to visit www.stickleyonsecurity.com for security tips and the latest alerts.